The Antiterrorism Handbook

The Antiterrorism Handbook

A Practical Guide to
Counteraction Planning and
Operations for Individuals,
Businesses, and Government

Karl A. Seger, Ph.D.

PRESIDIO

To Suzanne, Steven, and David. My life.

Published by Presidio Press
31 Pamaron Way, Novato, CA 94949

Library of Congress Cataloging-in-Publication Data

Seger, Karl A., 1940-
    The antiterrorism handbook: a practical guide to counteraction planning and operations for individuals, businesses, and government/Karl A. Seger.
        p. cm.
    ISBN 0-89141-369-3
    1. Terrorism—Prevention.   2. Terrorism—United States—Prevention.
I. Title
HV6431.S445 1990
363.3'2—dc20
                                                            90-6800
                                                            CIP

Printed in the United States of America

Contents

Acknowledgements

This book is the result of a collaborative effort involving the several thousand law enforcement officers, security professionals, and military personnel I have worked with in workshops, courses, and hands-on experiences during the past ten years. Each of these people asked questions and presented challenges that helped to develop the approaches to countering the threat of terrorism that are presented here.

The author owes special thanks to Col. James Fraser, U.S. Army, with whom I've had the opportunity to work on two unique projects: the development of T.C. 19-16, *Countering Terrorism on U.S. Army Installations* and the initial development of the Army Field Manual on terrorism counteraction. While we do not always agree on approaches to dealing with the problem of terrorism, we do agree on the need to listen and explore other points of view if our own thoughts and ideas are going to expand. Working with Jim is always a stimulating experience.

Preface

Terrorism is a problem that will continue to confront the nations of the world well into the next century. Although the problem itself has historical roots that date back to the beginning of man, contemporary terrorism presents challenges we have never before experienced.

This book does not attempt to outline solutions to the problem of terrorism. There is no one solution but rather a number of very complex approaches that have yet to be defined. My purpose here is to present antiterrorism approaches that can help to decrease the possibility of a terrorist or terrorist group successfully targeting the assets you are responsible for protecting. It is written for the soldiers, law enforcement officers, security professionals, and others who are responsible for preventing incidents from occurring and for responding when terrorists do strike. It will also provide information for the reader outside of the law enforcement and security communities who is trying to understand the problem of terrorism and our responses to it.

The first three chapters provide a basic understanding of the current problem and the concepts of terrorism counteraction and antiterrorism. Chapters Four through Eight discuss different steps to developing an effective antiterrorism, or prevention, program. Chapter Nine addresses some of the considerations of counterterrorism—the steps we must be prepared to take when responding to a terrorist incident.

This book is not intended to make you an expert in the antiterrorism areas that are discussed. But it should help to apply the expertise that you already have available from other sources to the problem of countering a terrorist attack. Physical security, for example, is a highly complex and technical area; it would require volumes of information to cover completely the application of physical security measures to antiterrorism. What I have attempted to provide here is an approach to applying known physical security measures to this particular area of concern.

A checklist for implementation procedures or key points is included at the end of each chapter. These should be helpful to trainers who will use this material to develop lesson plans for briefings and training sessions. They will also assist other personnel when implementing programs using the approaches that are presented.

Prologue

Enter Jack Pardue and the fictitious Aryan Peoples Party.

At the beginning of each chapter is a continuing scenario involving the town of Pleasantville, its key residents, and their adversaries. Jack Pardue is one of those adversaries. He is the leader of a white supremacist group that is dedicated to beginning Armageddon and to fulfilling what he perceives is an ordained mission. Although Jack is not a real person, there are people in the world who think exactly as he does and believe in the same things.

In the real world, groups operating in the United States have bombed, murdered, robbed, and committed other serious crimes. They have attempted to disrupt the electricity service to major urban areas and to poison the water supplies of cities such as Los Angeles. So, while the scenario is fictitious, it is not abstract. Many of the events detailed have already occurred, although under different circumstances.

The scenario will help you understand how to apply the concepts presented in each chapter. It also points out some of the realities of organizing and implementing a terrorism counteraction program. Unfortunately, in the real world, many programs are implemented as a knee-jerk response when a terrorist attack occurs. When nothing has happened for a while, the program is dismantled, leaving the organization a prime target for another attack.

Although the names of some groups and individuals in the scenario are real, all of the events are fictitious. The connection to the real-world names is used to demonstrate the potential for a similar situation to occur sometime in the future—perhaps in your community.

CHAPTER ONE

Understanding Contemporary Terrorism

SCENARIO

In his entire law enforcement career Charlie Fox had never received an assignment like this. Eighteen years ago he had left the Air Force after serving four years as a security police officer to join a civilian police department in the quiet community of Pleasantville. Since joining the department, he had been promoted through the ranks to his present position as deputy police chief of special projects. Several weeks ago his boss, Police Chief Phil Casey, had assigned Fox responsibility for forming a community threat management committee and for developing an intelligence capability to monitor potential terrorism and other subversive activities in the city.

Fox had never considered that terrorism could threaten his peaceful town. What surprised him the most about his new assignment was that the intelligence capability was already in place. He learned that the local offices of the Federal Bureau of Investigation (FBI) and the Bureau of Alcohol, Tobacco, and Firearms (BATF) were investigating the activities of a white supremacist group that had established a compound near Pleasantville. Both agencies believed that the leader of the Aryan Peoples Party, Jack Pardue, was living at the compound. Deputy Chief Fox had just received from these agencies a copy of an intelligence summary on the group and a sample of Jack Pardue's own writings. He sat down to read the intelligence report.

The Aryan Peoples Party (APP) was formed as an activist cell in 1985 after the Brotherhood of Silence, also known as the Order, failed in its attempt to overthrow the Zionist Occupational Government of the United States (ZOG).

All the members of the Order have either died in gun battles with the police or have been arrested and sentenced to long prison terms. The leader of the Order, Robert Mathews, who died during a shoot-out in Washington State, is considered by the leader of the APP, Jack Pardue, as a martyr and the only other person (besides Pardue) who had been capable and qualified to lead the Aryan resistance against ZOG.

Modeling itself after the Posse Comitatus (a right-wing survivalist group), the Aryan Peoples Party has established strategic compounds. Members of the group live on those compounds and spend most of their time there training in combat techniques and attending indoctrination sessions on Aryan supremacy. Unlike the Posse, however, all of the compounds are under the direction of Pardue, who serves as the Supreme Commander of the APP. Posse Comitatus compounds were each run by a local leader, and the eventual infighting between the leaders caused that movement to lose much of its effectiveness.

Pardue has structured the Aryan Peoples Party so as to provide within the group a base of active cadre who follow his orders explicitly. He has also taken advantage of the availability of former members of the Ku Klux Klan, Aryan Nation, and similar groups who provide the active and passive support needed to sustain the APP. Active supporters have purchased weapons and provided safe houses for the group. Passive supporters have solicited funds and conducted other legal activities in support of the Aryan movement.

During the past few years the APP has reportedly been contacted by other anti-Zionist movements around the world. The strangest of these contacts was initiated by a North African country run by a maniac colonel who offered state support for their activities. The initial gift to the group included a million dollars and four M-60 machine guns. According to intelligence sources, Pardue accepted the gifts, and he believes that these additional resources will help him not only to defeat ZOG but to eventually defeat the colonel and his nation as well. There are also reports that the APP has received support from neo-Nazi groups in Europe and, to a limited degree, from several Arab states that are dedicated to the destruction of Israel. This support has allowed the APP to purchase a vast arsenal of weapons and a supply of military explosives.

Group members have also planned and executed bank and armored car robberies. Their largest haul was an armored car robbery that netted more than $7 million, which was allegedly used to purchase M-79 grenade launchers and hand grenades from a black market connection operating out of Mexico. The publicity from these actions may have further increased the group's active and passive support network, with former members of the Posse Comitatus and various Ku Klux Klan groups providing the APP with additional money, safe houses, weapons, and other support.

The APP has been responsible for the bombing of federal buildings, synagogues, and several radio and television stations owned by Jewish interests. They murdered (or in their terms "assassinated") at least three people, including a Jewish radio personality who challenged them to "make me shut up," and a noted minority attorney who had filed several lawsuits against Aryan organizations, including Ku Klux Klan groups and the APP. All of these attacks and murders have been carried out with military precision, and none of the members responsible have been apprehended. The actions were probably preceded by extensive intelligence collection on the targets, but it is not known whether the APP maintains separate intelligence collection cells or if tactical personnel or active supporters are used for this purpose. It is suspected that these actions were planned by Jack Pardue and that the criminals responsible for carrying out Pardue's orders are hiding on APP compounds or in safe houses provided by active supporters of the organization.

The intelligence report left chills running up Charlie Fox's spine, especially when he read an additional entry that said the Aryan Peoples Party's compound was only twenty miles from Pleasantville. For the first time he honestly believed that terrorism might be a threat to his city.

Chief Fox then began reading from a recruiting pamphlet written by Jack Pardue:

Most of my predecessors in the Aryan movement have been dedicated but naive. From the early days of the Ku Klux Klan to the formation of the Posse Comitatus compounds and the Aryan Nation, many brave men have been drawn to the cause, but because their leaders failed them, they were unable to achieve their destiny. Those leaders failed to understand the divine nature of their mission, and they never fully comprehended the insidious cancer of Zionism and the effects of the mongrelization of the white race.

But as a prophet ordained by God himself, I, Jack Pardue, Supreme Commander of the Aryan Peoples Party, and a preacher in the Christian Identity Movement, understand our mission. The Aryan race is the true lost tribe of Israel, and the lands of America and the British Isles have been given to us by God. According to Identity doctrine, this is the message of Jesus Christ, and it is now up to us to fulfill God's plan. Armageddon is now, and the Aryan Peoples Party is leading the battle to overthrow the forces of Satan and to complete the prophecy of the movement.

Did Jack Pardue plan to begin Armageddon in Pleasantville? Only now did Fox realize how critical his new assignment could be. His community had never faced the threat of criminal activity from a terrorist group, and he wasn't sure they had the resources to respond if the APP targeted Pleasantville. Fox picked up the telephone and dialed Chief Casey's office.

* * *

Terrorism is not a new problem. The Zealots of Palestine used terrorist tactics in their struggle against the Roman occupation during the first century A.D. The Society of the Assassins (that is, the Hashshasin in tenth-century Persia) was a secret organization that was controlled by the mullahs and used to spread Islam throughout the Middle East by terrorizing their opponents. And our word "terrorism" is actually derived from the Reign of Terror that took place during the French Revolution in the 1790s.

Although terrorism is not a new problem, it is a phenomenon that has evolved into a highly developed strategy, allowing nations and in some cases small groups to conduct undeclared covert warfare. It is a strategy that is used against nations that are otherwise at peace. In areas experiencing extensive conflict, such as Lebanon, Afghanistan, and El Salvador, it has proven to be an effective tactic that is often used by both sides (or, in the case of Lebanon, all sides) of the conflict. Modern-day terrorists have moved beyond simple assassinations and bombings; they now have capabilities that provide them with the potential for killing thousands of people at a time and, as a result, threatening the political and economic stability of entire nations.

CATEGORIES OF TERRORIST GROUPS

There are three major categories of terrorist groups operating in the world today: nonstate-supported, state-sponsored, and state-directed groups.[1] (See Appendix A for a listing of today's major terrorist organizations.)

Nonstate-supported groups are small special-interest groups such as the antiabortionists, who blow up or set fire to abortion clinics, or the militant environmentalists, who set off bombs on utility towers constructed on land that the extremist group considers to be environmentally sensitive. Terrorist groups in this category usually have limited capabilities and do not have the infrastructure needed to maintain the group for a sustained period of time. They also do not have the contacts or support that groups in the other two categories enjoy, and their members are often caught because they lack the skills and training that international terrorists have received. However, a small, dedicated special-interest group that has proven its ability to generate widespread publicity for its cause may have the opportunity to make contact with groups in the other categories and as a result may find itself elevated from this status.

State-sponsored groups receive training, weapons, and other logistical and administrative support from sovereign nations such as Libya, Syria, Iran, Cuba, or countries of the Eastern bloc. Some of the training may take place in a third country away from the sponsoring state. The Eastern bloc, for example, has supported terrorist training throughout the Middle East in such places as Lebanon and South Yemen.

According to the U.S. Department of State, groups in this category are responsible for 70 percent of the international terrorist incidents targeted against Americans in the world today.[2] The support they receive from their sponsoring countries provides them with a unique capability to travel internationally, obtain sophisticated weapons and explosives, and coordinate their activities with other terrorist groups. Groups in Europe that have received support from the Eastern bloc, for example, banded together in the mid-1980s as an alliance and declared that they would engage in joint actions against NATO assets and other targets. Leftist groups in Latin America that receive support from Cuba have also shared weapons, explosives, and other resources.

Openly supporting terrorism can result in actions against the state sponsor. The U.S. bombing of Libya on April 14, 1986, and the economic sanctions that Britain called for against Syria that same year are examples of the risks these nations take. But as a result of these retaliatory actions, nations sponsoring terrorism simply continue to do so in a more covert manner. And when actions are taken against states that sponsor terrorism, those actions are not always condoned or supported by other countries. Almost every nation in the world condemned the United States for bombing Libya, and economic and diplomatic sanctions against states supporting terrorist groups have in most cases proven to be ineffective.

States that support terrorism do not always provide free handouts to the groups. In many cases the terrorists pay for their weapons, explosives, and even training. The sponsoring nations will encourage the group to use extortion, drug trafficking, kidnapping for ransom, bank robbery, and whatever other means are available to obtain the funds needed to support themselves. The sponsoring nation will then deliver the weapons and materials purchased by the group, using any means it has available, including its national airline or shipping service, or through the illegal use of diplomatic containers.

State-directed groups are organized, supplied, and controlled by a nation. In 1984 Iran decided to develop a 2,500-person special forces unit that would use terrorism as a primary tactic to spread its brand of Islamic fundamentalism throughout the Persian Gulf area and northern Africa.[3] The group was composed of young single men with combat experience who were each willing to undertake a suicide mission if commanded to do so. The extensive training they received was modeled primarily after the training given to Soviet Spetsnaz troops. Until recently Iran has been too bogged down by its war with Iraq to export this terrorism outside of the immediate region. Whether or not it will renew its commitment to this objective, now that the Iraq conflict is over, remains to be seen.

State-directed terrorists operating for nations in the Eastern bloc and other countries such as Libya have assassinated dissonant expatriated citizens around the world. North Korea used a team of state-directed assassins in 1983 to murder a number of South Korean officials visiting Rangoon and also to plant a bomb at Kimpo airport in Seoul. In 1985 in Miami, state-directed terrorists from Nicaragua attacked and beat a Roman Catholic cardinal who had been expelled from that country, warning him to stop speaking out against the Sandinista government.

The increase in state-sponsored and state-directed terrorism has significantly elevated the terrorist threat in our world. Most of today's groups are much better armed, trained, and supported than their predecessors.

GROUP ORGANIZATION

A terrorist movement must have effective leadership and an extensive support structure if it is to survive for any length of time. The leaders need to have dedicated followers within the group, and they need people outside of the terrorist group who will provide above-ground support such as intelligence collection and fund-raising. The two levels of group membership and both levels of supporters are shown in Figure 1–1.[4]

The hard-core leaders of the group are dedicated professionals. They are intelligent, charismatic, and often come from upper-income families. Some of these leaders had professional careers as physicians, attorneys, or writers. George Habash of the Popular Front for the Liberation of Palestine (PFLP) is an American University–trained physician; Bernadine Dohrn of the Weather Underground Organization (WUO) is a graduate of the University of Chicago Law School; and Ulrike Meinhof of the Baader-Meinhof was a talented leftist writer. In many groups, the leaders do not engage directly in the tactical operations but prefer to stay behind in their safe havens while sending other members to plant the bombs, conduct the assassinations, or take part in the attacks. Abu Nidal prefers the safety of Damascus and his other havens to participation in his group's attacks in Rome, Vienna, or other parts of the world. Abu el-Abbas was not present on the *Achille Lauro* nor has he taken part in the numerous other actions within Israel for which his group has been responsible.

There are some exceptions to the "stay at home" style of terrorist group leadership. Robert Mathews, who formed the Brotherhood of Silence, the most active terrorist group in the United States during 1984 and 1985, conducted some of their early bank robberies by himself to raise money for the group. Mathews further demonstrated his commitment to the cause when he chose to die as a martyr rather than surrender when surrounded by federal agents at a safe house on Whidbey Island in Puget Sound. At least two members of the group escaped and three others were arrested during that incident.

Since most terrorist leaders do not participate in the tactical operations, the real doers in the groups are the active cadre. These are the people who conduct most of the intelligence missions, build and plant the bombs, and are responsible for the attacks and assassinations. Some of the members

Figure 1-1
TERRORIST ORGANIZATION AND SUPPORT STRUCTURE

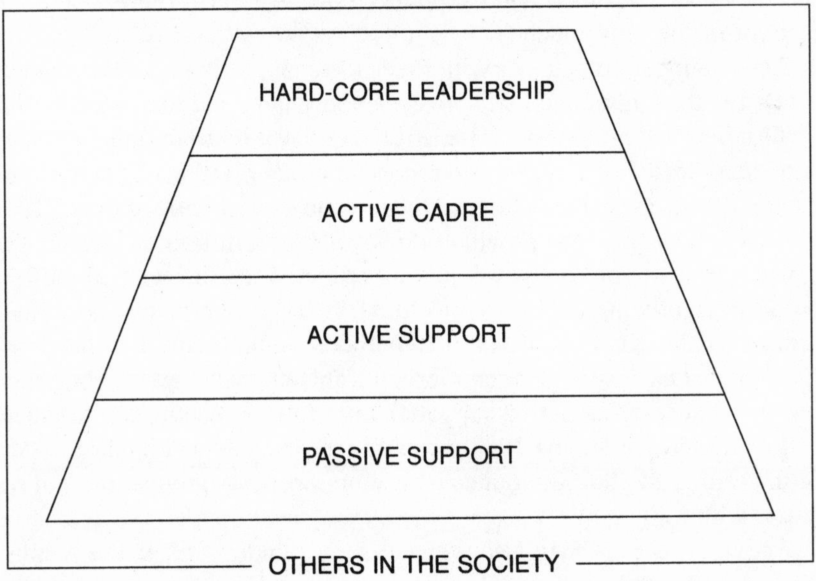

in this category are specialists in their respective areas, whereas others may be assigned operational duties based on the needs of the group at that particular time. For example, Marwan Yusuf al-Banna, an Abu Nidal Group member, was originally placed in London as a one-person intelligence cell, but he was subsequently ordered by his contact at the Syrian Embassy to assassinate the Israeli ambassador. Al-Banna was captured by British police after the attempted assassination on 3 June 1982.

Although many terrorist leaders are highly intelligent and fall well within the normal ranges on most psychological scales, the active cadre group may include sociopaths and individuals suffering from inadequate personality development. This is in part due to the fact that some groups recruit active cadre members who are in prison for other crimes. Donald DeFreeze of the Symbionese Liberation Army (SLA) became a "revolutionary" while incarcerated at San Quentin, and Gary Yarbrough became associated with right-wing extremism as a result of the Aryan Nation prison ministry program. He joined that group, and eventually the Brotherhood of Silence, immediately after being released from prison in Arizona. Association with a terrorist organization provides these individuals with an accepted outlet (by their standards) for their violent sociopathic tendencies.

For the terrorist organization to survive it must also include active and passive supporters. These people are not actually members of the group but they are sympathetic and supportive of the espoused credo and objectives of the movement.

Active supporters interact with the leaders and the cadre. They collect funds for the cause, publish above-ground papers and manifestos, rent safe houses, and provide other logistical and administrative support. These supporters include attorneys who represent group members when they are captured, and physicians who treat them while they are underground. They also include people who provide safe havens for terrorists on the run. An extensive network of active supporters provided housing and other basic needs to right-wing extremists in the U.S. who were members of such groups as the Ku Klux Klan, Brotherhood of Silence, and the Posse Comitatus. One Posse member, Gordon Kahl, was surrounded while staying in a house of an active supporter in the Ozark section of Arkansas and died there on 3 June 1983 when a tear-gas grenade detonated some of the estimated 100,000 rounds of ammunition that he had stored in the house with him.

Active supporters may also form above-ground organizations to raise funds for the terrorist cause. In some cases, people contributing to these organizations do not know what the funds will actually be used for. In 1979, during the Iranian revolution, an organization in the United States raised money from unsuspecting donors and funneled those funds to a group in Iran that was responsible for the murder of several Americans. More recently, a group operating in the United States has been collecting funds for medical aid to victims of the guerrilla war in El Salvador. The organization has collected millions of dollars and was even able to solicit the support of several members of Congress to help them raise money. However, according to the intelligence community, most of the money raised was actually used, and continues to be used, by the Frente Farabundo Marti De Liberacion Nacional (FMLN) Communist insurgents and terrorists in El Salvador to buy weapons and other items needed to fill their logistical needs.

People who support the announced cause of the terrorist organization but will not openly involve themselves in criminal activities are passive supporters. These are the individuals who contribute money, who loan active supporters or other people the keys to their beach house or car without asking any questions, or who collect information that may be important to the terrorist intelligence collection activities.

As shown in Figure 1–2, each cell within the actual terrorist group (that is, the hard-core leadership and active cadre) has a specialized function.[5] The command cell consists of the leadership, who as we have already discussed may not take part in the group's intelligence collection or tactical activities. The command cell functions just as the upper-level management of any major organization does, directing the activities of others. In fact, since many groups have annual budgets that exceed a million dollars, and in several cases are well over $10 million, the annual cash flow of these organizations is larger than that of many legitimate businesses in the world. In the larger terrorist groups the cells perform the same specialized functions as illustrated for the smaller groups, but by necessity there are more cells and there is an extended command and control structure.

There are a number of intelligence cells from the same group operating in the field at any given time. The leaders order members to collect information on general targets, such as all of the Jewish or minority leadership (depending on the credo of the group) in an area. In some cases they may assign specific targets for intelligence collection, such as an embassy, military installation, or a Fortune 500 company. The intelligence collected by these cells will then be delivered to the command cell and used to evaluate and select targets.

The support-section cells take care of the logistical needs of the group

Figure 1-2
TERRORIST GROUP STRUCTURE

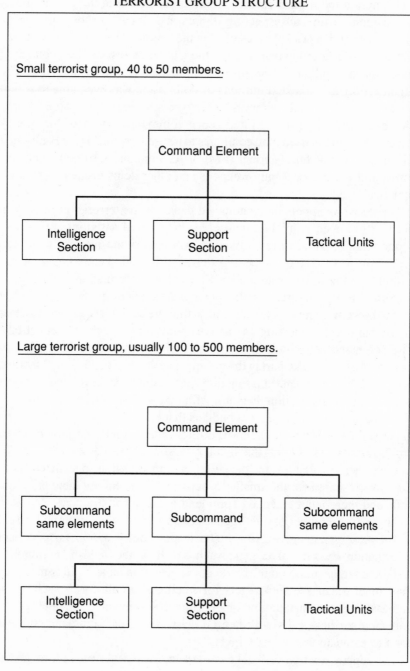

members. They rent the safe houses, purchase the groceries, and procure arms, ammunition, and explosives. Members of the support cells may also interact with the active supporters who assist in providing these materials and funds.

Although a larger terrorist group will have a number of intelligence and support cells in operation at all times, for security reasons there may be only a limited number of tactical cells in the field. In some cases a group member or cell performing another function (for example, intelligence or support) may be activated as a tactical cell, as the Abu Nidal Group did with Marwan Yusuf Muhmud al-Banna. In other cases, members assigned to the tactical cells may be housed in terrorist training camps in the Middle East, Cuba, the Eastern bloc, or North Korea for an extended period of time while their leaders are deciding on the target they will be assigned upon completion of their training. Kim Hyon Hui, a member of the Japanese Red Army, remained in a North Korean training camp for eight years before receiving orders to plant a bomb on a South Korean civilian airliner. The bomb killed 115 people.

Members of the tactical cells are the people who set off the bombs, commit the assassinations, and carry out the kidnappings, hijackings, hostage-takings, and other spectacular actions of the group. Some of these members are so dedicated to the group cause that they are willing to participate in suicide missions. Others may be sent out on a suicide mission by the leadership without being told about it, if the leaders have decided that the short-term objective achieved as a result of the action is worth more than the lives of the tactical cell members.

PHASES OF A TERRORIST INCIDENT

Terrorist incidents are well planned, they are often rehearsed, and they are usually carried out with military precision. As shown in Figure 1–3, there are four or five distinct phases to each incident.[6]

The intelligence needed to plan the event is collected during the preincident phase by one of the group's intelligence cells. This information is communicated to the command cell for target selection and the development of the plan of attack. A tactical cell may rehearse the incident during this phase while the intelligence unit continues to observe the target. Not only are the intelligence collection, rehearsal, and attack usually conducted by different cells within the group, but in a few cases these

Figure 1-3
PHASES OF A TERRORIST INCIDENT

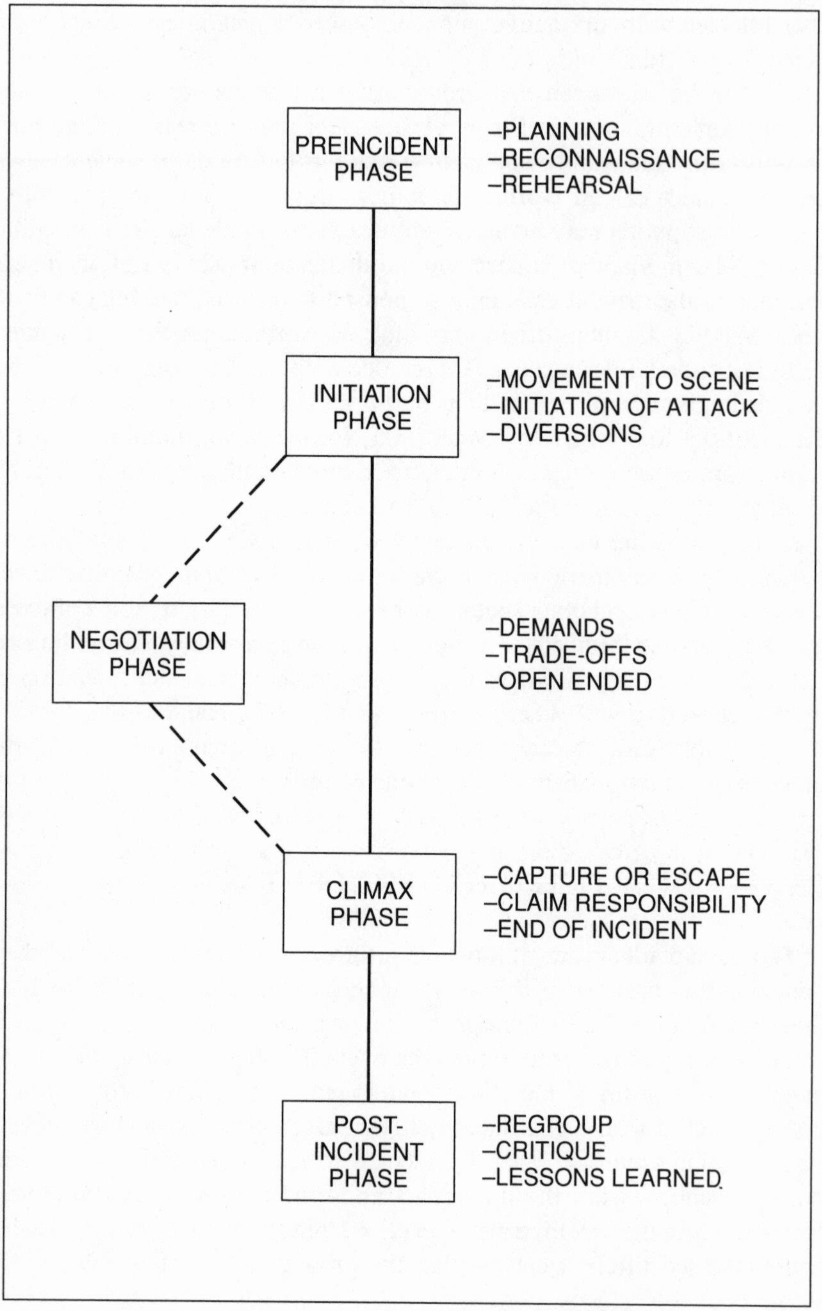

PREINCIDENT PHASE	−PLANNING −RECONNAISSANCE −REHEARSAL
INITIATION PHASE	−MOVEMENT TO SCENE −INITIATION OF ATTACK −DIVERSIONS
NEGOTIATION PHASE	−DEMANDS −TRADE-OFFS −OPEN ENDED
CLIMAX PHASE	−CAPTURE OR ESCAPE −CLAIM RESPONSIBILITY −END OF INCIDENT
POST-INCIDENT PHASE	−REGROUP −CRITIQUE −LESSONS LEARNED.

activities have been conducted by members of different groups. The May 1982 attack on Lod Airport (now Ben Gurian Airport) in Israel was planned and rehearsed by members of the PFLP. However, the actual attack, during which twenty-six people died and seventy-two were injured, was conducted by members of the Japanese Red Army. The leaders of the two groups met at a training camp in North Korea and decided to conduct the joint operation to demonstrate solidarity among anti-imperialist, anti-Zionist movements around the world.

Once the leaders have selected a target and developed an attack plan, the tactical cell is activated. This begins the initiation phase of the incident. The members of the tactical cell may travel to the target using different routes and then come together only at the last minute. They prefer to pick up their weapons and explosives once they reach the target area rather than carry them as they travel to help avoid detection while en route. Diversionary tactics are often employed to mask the identity of the primary target. Bombs may be detonated to attract security forces to one area while the group kidnaps a victim located some miles away. Or a bomb threat may be called in at one location while the terrorists plant the actual bombs somewhere else. They also use this diversionary tactic to draw police or military personnel into the open for an ambush. The group will telephone a bomb threat to the police station, knowing the route the officers will take to the suspected bomb scene, and then ambush them while they are en route.

If the incident is a hostage-taking or kidnapping event, the negotiation phase comes next. The terrorists make their demands known, and the authorities then attempt to bargain for the lives of the victims and the surrender of the group members. During the 1970s, authorities developed and honed the techniques of hostage negotiation into a fine art. Unfortunately, terrorists have since "read the book" and have changed their tactics. As a result, some of the hostage-negotiation techniques that have worked in the past are no longer effective when we are confronted by a hard-core terrorist cell. The problem of attempting to negotiate with a political hostage-taker is increased even further when we are dealing with terrorists who desire to die during the event or with others who simply refuse to talk directly to a negotiator, making the traditional approaches to negotiation almost useless. In most cases the negotiation is settled in favor of the terrorists since in almost 90 percent of these events the group achieves its immediate goal of publicity and all of the terrorists escape or are released.[7]

The climax phase is when the bomb goes off, the attack takes place, the victim is assassinated, or the hostage event is terminated. At this point the terrorists either escape or are killed or captured. If the incident is a bombing, the terrorists may be hundreds or even thousands of miles away when the detonation occurs, and they can claim responsibility for the attack via a long-distance telephone call to the location where the explosion occurred or to a media source where their safe house or headquarters is located.

Terrorist groups usually do an excellent job of developing their after-action and lessons-learned reports during the post-incident phase. The group leaders evaluate what went right with the operation, what went wrong, and how they can improve their tactics and strategy for the next bombing or attack. Groups even call upon outside "experts" to evaluate their operations and make recommendations for the future. After the initial South Moluccan hostage-taking incidents in Holland, during the 1970s, the Moluccans called upon several outsiders, including the now-deceased Carlos (Ilich Ramirez Sanchez) to critique their operation. As a result, their next hostage-taking event was much more professional and deadly.

Terrorists are very careful while planning the event and executing their plan to insure the highest possible probability of success. The leaders are well qualified to plan each phase of the operation, and once they are committed, the highly trained tactical cells are dedicated to accomplishing the objectives of the mission.

CONTEMPORARY FACTORS

Although terrorism is a problem that has plagued humanity for centuries, there are at least nine factors that make contemporary terrorism a unique phenomenon. They are:

1. State sponsorship of terrorist groups.
2. Impact of the modern media.
3. Today's improved communication capabilities.
4. Domestic and international transportation.
5. Intergroup cooperation.
6. The possibility of suicide missions.
7. Some terrorists' desire (not just willingness) to die.
8. Potential for megaterrorism.
9. State-sponsored retaliatory acts for money.

We have already discussed the impact of **state sponsorship.** Groups in this category are better trained, they have access to highly sophisticated equipment, and they may be receiving intelligence and other support formerly available only to espionage agents or the military of their sponsoring nation.

Every terrorist event is a **media** event. With the impact of television and the instant communications available to both the electronic and print media, the old Chinese saying "Kill one and frighten ten thousand" can be rewritten to read "Kill one and frighten ten million." When an American terrorist blew up the governor of Idaho in 1905, it took days for news of the assassination to reach around the world. But when a group of hijackers took over a Pan American jet on the ground in Karachi in 1986, people in the United States could actually see the airplane on the ground as they watched the morning news.

People who claim that the problem of terrorism is sensationalized because more people die on the highways every year than have been killed by terrorists in the past two decades do not understand the dynamics of the problem. Terrorism is not measured in body counts, by the number of wounded, or by the dollar value of the damages. Terrorism is measured in terms of the column inches in newspapers and magazines and the number of minutes an event generates on television and radio. Almost every terrorist event is a media event, and the media love it. After every major terrorist event (and especially after a prolonged hostage-taking incident), authorities cry for the need for media guidelines to prevent the vulturelike, sometimes obscene behavior of the media that occurred during the event. Sometimes the media even agrees to the establishment of a general set of guidelines; that is until the next event occurs. Then the vultures reappear and all restraint is lost.

Consider the behavior of the media during the TWA 847 incident in 1985. There was a television journalist interviewing two brothers whose father was on the hijacked plane, asking how they felt about the situation! Remember, too, the press conference staged by the Amal Militia during which the media was so ill-behaved that even the terrorists were upset and moved the conference to a larger room where they could exercise more control. What the press failed to report regarding that press conference was that each of the media presented paid for the right to be there, up to $12,500 each, according to some sources.[8] We have reached the point where the media now provides financial as well as moral support for terrorist movements.

Terrorist group members are able to communicate with each other, with their leaders, and with their state sponsors using **modern communication** equipment. This may be as simple as placing a long-distance telephone call, or it may include the use of sophisticated electronic communication devices such as those used by government intelligence agencies. Groups have even communicated information to each other and their supporters using computer networks. This improved communication capability makes it possible for the leaders to direct their tactical cells during the operation and for last-minute intelligence information to be shared by group members.

Today's **transportation** capabilities provide contemporary terrorists with the means of planting a bomb in Paris and flying back to Beirut as it explodes. State-sponsored terrorists can strike at a declared adversary anywhere in the world, and even domestic terrorists rely on modern transportation as part of their plans. In the United States, groups spend a great deal of time traveling the interstate highways. Members of the United Freedom Front (see Appendix A) maintained residences in Ohio, leaving every Monday morning to rob banks, collect intelligence, and bomb targets in New Jersey, New York, Connecticut, and Massachusetts. They would then return home on Friday and enjoy a typical suburban family weekend. Terrorists belonging to the right-wing Brotherhood of Silence, using vans and motor homes as safe houses, traveled the interstate highways across the United States. When a Missouri Highway Patrol officer stopped David Tate's van on April 15, 1985, for a routine traffic check, Tate, a member of the Order, killed the officer and wounded his partner. Inside the van, police found an arsenal of weapons, scanners, and other tactical equipment.

There has also been an increase in **intergroup cooperation.** In the U.S., members of the Weather Underground Organization, Black Liberation Party, Republic of New Africa, and the Black Panthers came together to form the Revolutionary Armed Task Force (RATF). The RATF was responsible for an armored car robbery at Nyack, New York, during which three people were murdered. In Europe, the Red Army Faction (Federal Republic of Germany), Action Direct (France), and the Communist Combatant Cells (Belgium) announced that they would be working together on joint operations and in mutual support of each other. The sharing between groups of information, arms, explosives, and other materials greatly enhances the capabilities of the groups involved in the alliance.

Suicide missions are also a factor today. When evaluating the intelligence on a potential target, the last thing considered by the group leaders is the possibility of escape by the tactical cell. If the immediate objectives of the operation (for example, publicity for the cause, retaliation for a previous event) warrant, the leadership may commit the cell knowing that they have little chance for survival. In some cases the cell is not told it is being sent on a suicide mission or that the cell members are being sacrificed for the cause.

However, some terrorists are not only willing to die, but they actually **desire to die** for their cause. This is a new twist that is associated with the Shiites, but to a lesser degree occurs in other categories of terrorists (both Robert Mathews of the Order and Gordon Kahl of the Posse Comitatus made conscious decisions to become martyrs). A few of these people may be so committed to the cause that they are willing to sacrifice themselves, but most are either coerced into suicide missions (for example, with a threat to their family), or they are high on drugs when sent out on a mission. While the Koran prohibits the use of alcohol, the culture from which many Middle Eastern terrorists are recruited accepts, and may even encourage, the use of hashish and other drugs.

Another concern regarding contemporary terrorism is the **potential for megaterrorism,** which refers to the possibility of terrorists using a weapon or tactic that could kill thousands of people. Police in France raided a terrorist safe house where a botulism agent was being manufactured for use by the Red Army Faction in West Germany.[9] Eight ounces of the agent would be enough to kill every human being on earth. In the United States, the Weather Underground planned to steal nerve gas from a military site in New Jersey and release it in New York City. The action was prevented when an informant notified a federal agency of the plan. In another case, the Order of the Rising Star, a neo-Nazi group, manufactured eighty pounds of typhoid bacilli on their own. They intended to release the agent in the water supplies of several midwestern cities. In North Carolina another group successfully sabotaged the water supply of a small community, forcing the city to truck in all of its water until the problem could be corrected.

Much has been written about the potential for a nuclear terrorist event. Terrorists could steal a nuclear device or they might receive a nuclear weapon from a state sponsor. The possibility that they could manufacture a device on their own is very small. But just the threat of a nuclear incident has forced the U.S. and other governments to form special teams to respond if such an event should occur. This threat recently increased when it was discovered that a group in southern Europe is attempting to manufacture ready-made nuclear devices for sale to any terrorist group or nation that can afford them.[10]

Megaterrorism is a real threat. The Palestinian groups are raising a new generation of terrorists who are much more committed to their cause than terrorists were a decade ago. The refusal of Israel to cooperate in the establishment of a Palestinian homeland, and that country's move to establish new settlements on the West Bank and other territories, has removed almost any hope that Palestinians had for a negotiated settlement. This can only lead to more terrorism and the potential use of megaterrorism tactics in that part of the world. There is a high degree of probability that Shiite terrorists would use megaterrorism in their commitment to spread Islamic fundamentalism. And in America, right-wing extremists believe that Armageddon is already here; they could conceivably escalate their tactics to include megaterrorism to help that process along. Some of these terrorists have already received training in chemical and biological warfare, and it is only a matter of time before they put this training to use.

Pan American Flight 103, the airplane that was destroyed in December 1988, may be an example of the final contemporary trend in terrorism: **a state-sponsored event committed for money.** A total of 270 people died when a bomb exploded on the aircraft, sending it plunging to the ground at Lockerbie, Scotland. Warnings that a terrorist bomb may have been placed on an aircraft were issued by the British government on 22 November 1988 and 19 December 1988, the final warning coming just two days before the tragic incident occurred.

One of the groups that may have been responsible for the bombing, the Popular Front for the Liberation of Palestine–General Command, could have planted the bomb under contract to Libya in retaliation for the U.S. air raid over that country, or the group may have been paid by the Iranians, who wanted revenge for the accidental shooting down of an Iranian civilian airplane in the summer of 1988. In either case, we have a terrorist group committing an extremely violent act for mercenary reasons. This expands the concept of using terrorism as a medium of covert warfare; we now have groups committing acts for state sponsors specifically designed to satisfy the short-term goals of the state rather than the group.

WHERE TO FROM HERE?

Contemporary terrorism is a mode of warfare. It is a strategy and tactic that allows nations to commit covert acts of war against other states and even permits small groups to go to war with sovereign nations. Libya and

Iran are able to take on the United States by sponsoring terrorism against U.S. targets while disavowing any connection with the groups responsible for the attacks. Small groups such as the United Freedom Front can dedicate themselves to the overthrow of the U.S. government, while their right-wing counterparts, the Brotherhood of Silence, signed their own declaration of war against ZOG, the Zionist Occupational Government of the United States. The Red Army Faction can maintain its conflict with the government of West Germany, and the Irish Republican Army (IRA) and the Provos can continue to hit at British targets as their 600-year-old war continues.

The ultimate example of the use of terrorism as a medium of warfare in a low-intensity conflict environment was the bombing of the Marine Landing Team barracks in Beirut on 23 October 1983. The attack was probably coordinated, if not directed, by Iran, which has never been held responsible for the 241 deaths caused by the massive car bombing. The objective of the event was to get the Americans out of Lebanon. Does terrorism work as a tactic in covert warfare? How many Marines are in the peacekeeping force in Lebanon today?

Another continuing threat is the use of terrorism by special-interest groups. Abortion clinic bombers will continue their attacks. Persons opposed to nuclear weapons or to U.S. policy in Central America, and individuals motivated by other issues, will use terrorist tactics to gain media attention for their causes.

It appears that the terrorism problem will get worse before it gets better. Governments in the free world still do not understand the phenomenon of international terrorism or how to deal with it. In spite of all the rhetoric following every major attack against U.S. interests, the U.S. has been almost impotent in dealing with the problem. The Carter administration failed to understand the options available during the Iranian hostage crisis. President Reagan's most dramatic response has been the air attack on Libya, for which almost every nation in the world condemned the United States. Britain has attempted to impose diplomatic and economic sanctions against Syria for its involvement in state-sponsored terrorism in England, but has failed to gain any real support among other nations. Israel has a dedicated policy of retaliation against terrorists, but groups continue to hit Israeli targets and Jewish interests around the world.

There have, however, been isolated successes by law enforcement agencies in their battle against terrorism. The U.S. Department of Justice and the FBI have proven to be highly effective in combating some domestic terrorist groups. After a New Jersey State Highway Patrol officer arrested Ya Kikumura during a routine traffic stop in April 1988, the government was able to prosecute him for having three pipe bombs in his possession. Kikumura is a member of the Japanese Red Army, and it is believed he was on his way to plant the bombs in a federal building in New York where a Navy recruiting station is located. The bombs were to be exploded on April 14, the anniversary of the U.S. air strike on Libya. Kikumura was sentenced to 30 years in prison.

In September 1987 the FBI was able to entice a Lebanese Shiite terrorist, Fawaz Younis, to board a yacht in international waters off Cyprus, where he was arrested and promptly brought to the U.S. for trial. Younis was accused of hijacking a Royal Jordanian airliner in 1985, which had two Americans among the passengers. He was convicted under a 1984 federal law that makes it a federal crime to commit a hijacking anywhere in the world if Americans are among the victims.

These successes are sending a clear message to the active cadre terrorists around the world. They can be made to pay for their crimes.

KEY POINTS

1. Categories of terrorist groups include:
   a. Nonstate supported.
   b. State sponsored.
   c. State directed.
2. Terrorist organization and support structure.
   a. Hard-core leaders.
   b. Active cadre.
   c. Active supporters.
   d. Passive supporters.
3. Phases of a terrorist incident.
   a. Preincident phase.
   b. Initiation phase.
   c. Negotiation phase.
   d. Climax phase.
   e. Post-incident phase.
4. Contemporary terrorism factors.
   a. State sponsorship of terrorist groups.
   b. Impact of the modern media.
   c. Today's improved communication capabilities.
   d. Domestic and international transportation.
   e. Intergroup cooperation.
   f. The possibility of suicide missions.
   g. Some terrorists' desire (not just willingness) to die.
   h. Potential for megaterrorism.
   i. State-sponsored retaliatory acts for money.

CHAPTER TWO

Terrorism Counteraction

SCENARIO

"Chief, this is Charlie Fox. I've been reviewing some information on the group that set up the compound about twenty miles from here and I think we'd better take a closer look at the situation. When can we get together?"

"You mean the Aryan Peoples Party? I'll tell you something, Charlie, I just read the FBI report on that group and they have me concerned too. How about two o'clock?"

Fox sat back in his chair, making some notes on a yellow legal pad for his meeting with the chief. He realized that if he was going to fully understand and be able to manage this threat, he needed to stop thinking like Charlie Fox and learn to think like Jack Pardue. He had never dealt with someone as committed to his cause as Pardue was to Aryan supremacy. Charlie thought about the community he was charged with protecting, and he wondered why Pardue had chosen Pleasantville.

Located in the rolling hills of mid-America, Pleasantville was a typical small town. It provided all the advantages of small-town life, yet was close to a major urban area with its cultural, shopping, and educational opportunities. But to Charlie the greatest asset of Pleasantville was its warm and friendly people.

Pleasantville also enjoyed a stable economic base. The two major employers in the town were a U.S. military research and development center and a major chemical plant. Perhaps this attracted Pardue, Charlie thought. The military installation, Fort Richardson, conducted research on chemical and biological weapons and on the countermeasures that can be used against these agents. The installation employed a number of high-level scientists and attracted visitors from around the world. The chemical plant, Toten Industries, had been recently awarded a new five-year contract by the Department of Defense and was adding an additional 100 people to its payroll.

Burke Wilson was mayor of Pleasantville. He also owned a local insurance agency. He had been mayor for the past twenty years, having been reelected every four years since he first took office. Burke was born and raised in Pleasantville and he was the town's best spokesperson, constantly promoting the advantages of living in a small community and bragging about the people of Pleasantville. He was proud of the fact that his town was a model example of affirmative action and that people of all races and creeds lived together in harmony. Pleasantville's government was based on the New England concept of monthly town meetings that encouraged all citizens to take an active part in community affairs and decisions.

Pleasantville could also be proud of its effective police department. Police Chief Phillip Casey had come up through the ranks of the seventy-five-person department, starting as a patrol officer fifteen years ago. When the last chief retired just two years ago, everyone in the community felt that Phil was the right man for the job. He was an educated, trained professional who worked well with the officials in city government, the members of his department, and the people in the community. He maintained close contacts with the commander at Fort Richardson, the president of Toten Industries, and with their security directors as well. Charlie Fox had also been considered for the chief's job, but he was content to stay in his current position. He liked what he was doing, and he wasn't sure he wanted to play the political games that usually go with the chief's rank and responsibilities.

The police department had a reputation for maintaining an excellent crime prevention program: Crime statistics in Pleasantville were well below the averages for the region and the nation. But in the past the department had to deal only with "normal" categories of crime. Now it seemed that the community was being confronted by politically motivated criminals or, as the media preferred to call them, terrorists. According to everything Fox had heard or read, terrorists were in most cases more professional and much more committed than ordinary criminals.

In addition to his concern about the Aryan Peoples Party, Charlie Fox was thinking also about the negative publicity that Fort Richardson and Toten Industries had been receiving lately. An international group opposed to the development and production of chemical and biological weapons had threatened to come to Pleasantville to organize demonstrations and form a local chapter of Citizens Against Chemical Warfare. So far the group had been nonviolent, although a number of its members had been arrested for criminal trespassing during demonstrations. The group was based in Washington, D.C. but, according to an FBI intelligence report, it could be a Soviet Front group that received its support and encouragement through the Cuban Intelligence Service, the DGI.

At the appointed time, Fox walked into the meeting and found that Chief Casey had invited Mayor Wilson to join them.

The mayor rose to shake his hand. "Charlie, I understand you have some concerns that I should hear about."

The chief greeted Fox, then sat back down, turning over the meeting to him. Charlie began his presentation.

"Here's the problem, Mayor. A group known as the Aryan Peoples Party has established a compound about twenty miles from Pleasantville and we think they may be planning some kind of action. Also, a Washington-based group, the Citizens Against Chemical Warfare, is trying to start a chapter here. But my major concern is that our department is not ready to deal with any type of political crime or demonstrations. I think we need to upgrade our capabilities in these areas."

"What exactly are you proposing?" asked the mayor.

Fox responded. "As remote as this may seem, I think we need to establish a terrorism counteraction program with both antiterrorism and counterterrorism components. We're already doing fairly well with our counterterrorism capabilities. The department has a four-person bomb squad trained at Red Stone Arsenal and a six-person tactical unit trained at the FBI school at Quantico. But these officers are assigned to regular patrol duties and perform their functions as bomb technicians or tactical officers only when there is a call-out. Frankly, Mayor, it would be hard to cost-justify a full-time tactical force for a department our size. What I think we need to develop is a contingency plan to put these people on full alert when the threat reaches a certain level, even if nothing has happened yet. As of now, we can't accomplish this.

"My major concern is in the area of antiterrorism. This includes the actions we can take to prevent, deter, or predict a terrorist criminal act in our community and to maintain intelligence on groups such as the Aryan Peoples Party. The best way to achieve this objective is to form a community-wide threat management committee that includes representatives from the appropriate federal and state agencies, and also from Fort Richardson and Toten Industries."

Chief Casey smiled. When he assigned Fox the responsibility for forming the threat management committee, Charlie had thought the chief was overreacting. Now it was *Charlie* who was trying to sell the concept to the mayor.

"A community-wide threat management committee," Fox went on, "would allow us to draw upon all the available resources needed to monitor the situation and combat potential terrorist problems such as demonstrations, bombings, even assassinations and kidnappings."

Obviously Fox had gotten Mayor Wilson's attention. But the mayor was a politician, and his reaction was predictable.

"Look, Charlie," the mayor interrupted, "you've done your homework on this, and I'll go along with the formation of the committee. Just make sure you keep me informed on the committee's actions and concerns. But there is something else you need to keep in mind too. This is an election year, and I learned a long time ago that it's best to keep potentially negative information out of the press and to control the city's budget if you want to get reelected. So keep this committee thing low key and remember that there's no additional money in this year's budget for more police officers or special equipment. And don't let this intelligence thing get out of hand. I don't want to hear about the department bugging some council person's office or infiltrating some citizen group. Let's try to keep it all in perspective."

As Mayor Wilson walked out of the office, Chief Casey felt that they had accomplished something: At least the mayor now was aware of the potential problem. Charlie Fox wasn't quite as satisfied. He believed that the mayor was simply trying to placate them.

*   *   *

Terrorism is a phenomenon that is easier to describe than to define.[1] In fact, preparing a concise definition of terrorism, to which all governments and agencies within those governments can agree, is analogous to the old story about the three blind men attempting to describe an elephant while each man was touching a different part of the animal's body. Each blind man described a very different animal. The same thing happens when different agencies or organizations attempt to define terrorism. Each definition will reflect the mission and the immediate concerns of the agency preparing it. For our purposes, we will use the following general definition:

> Terrorism is the use of violence or the threat of violence for political purposes by individuals or groups, whether acting for, or in opposition to,

established government authority when such actions are intended to influence a target group beyond the immediate victim or victims.[2]

The key elements of this definition are: 1. terrorism is a political act; 2. it includes the use of violence or the threat of violence; and 3. it is intended to influence an audience beyond the immediate victim(s).

Efforts to manage the threat of terrorism are categorized according to three definitions.[3]

Antiterrorism includes all of the actions taken to prevent terrorism or a specific terrorist act from occurring. These actions include threat assessments, target hardening, personal protection, and operations security.

Counterterrorism is the response to an actual terrorist event. This includes the tactical response, the criminal investigation, and the emergency operations command and control structure that manages the response to an ongoing terrorist situation such as a hostage-taking or kidnapping event.

Terrorism counteraction is the umbrella term used to describe all antiterrorism and counterterrorism measures. These include the actions taken by governments to counteract the threat, including specific measures initiated by military units or installations, law enforcement agencies, and security professionals to decrease the probability of an attack against a specific asset. It also includes the actions taken in response to an event, from the use of a tactical team during a hostage-taking situation to the retaliatory bombing of a nation that sponsors a specific event or group.

TERRORISM COUNTERACTION MIND-SET

Before you can begin to intuitively comprehend the steps that need to be taken to manage this threat, you must first develop a **terrorism counteraction mind-set**. People within the terrorism infrastructure do not think the way most of us think. They are fanatically committed to their cause, and they earnestly believe that every possible tactic and means are justified in achieving their goals, including the murder of old people, women, children, and babies.

We all have our own ethnocentric limitations, that is, the set of values and beliefs we develop as we mature in our own cultural setting. However, if we are going to understand the different forms of terrorism in the world today, we must learn to shed our own ethnocentric qualities and attempt to assume the mind-set of the adversary. This challenge is magnified by the fact that each of the major groups in the world has a different set of motivations, beliefs, and values. In the 1970s, for example, terrorism counteraction planners were confronted primarily by left-wing terrorism in the United States, Latin American terrorists, and Palestinian groups attacking Israeli targets. As we evolved into the 1980s the threat changed. Palestinians are now attacking targets around the world and not all of them are Israeli. The major groups operating in the U.S. have been right-wing extremists associated with the neo-Nazi Aryan supremacy movements. And although Latin America still has its share of terrorism, the Shiites of the Middle East have captured the primary attention of terrorism counteraction agencies around the world. Groups such as the Red Army Faction have proven to be much more resilient and professional than their Baader-Meinhof predecessor, and international groups such as the Japanese Red Army have matured into deadly adversaries that have proven their ability to operate on at least four continents.

The antiterrorism and terrorism counteraction planner must learn to think like a terrorist! This person must understand that a terrorist is willing to murder innocent civilians, is totally committed to his cause, and may be willing to die for what he perceives as the "greater cause." The planner must adapt to the mind-set of the groups that present a threat to the assets he is responsible for protecting. He must be aware of the tactics they use, the training they have received, and the operational patterns they follow.

Once you develop the ability to think like a terrorist, then you can begin to think like a terrorism counteraction planner. At this point you are ready to assess the degree of the threat to your assets and evaluate your vulnerabilities. All of these actions are taken as you develop the threat analysis discussed in Chapter Five.

After your threat analysis is developed and the antiterrorism program is in place, then expect the unexpected! You must assume that your terrorist adversary will continue to develop intelligence on your activities, looking for weaknesses and vulnerabilities. If you develop procedures to keep out bombs, then the terrorist might decide to use rocket launchers or mortars to attack you. If your key personnel are all secure, then expect the group to attempt to assassinate or kidnap someone else in the organization. Obviously it is almost impossible to totally secure most facilities, which is why you must try to stay one step ahead of whatever the other side may be planning.

BASIC OBJECTIVES

The four basic objectives of most government terrorism counteraction programs are prevention, deterrence, reaction, and prediction. Reaction is a counterterrorism activity, whereas the other three objectives are antiterrorism considerations.

Prevention is achieved through international initiatives and diplomacy. Ideally, all nations of the world would agree that terrorism is wrong and join together to combat it. But this will never happen. Consider the old cliché that "one man's terrorist is another man's freedom fighter." The Palestinian groups may be considered terrorists by the Israelis and other nations they have targeted, but they are viewed as heroes and fedayeen (fighters willing to sacrifice themselves for the cause) by most of the displaced Palestinians in the world, and they are considered legitimate military units by many of the world's nations.

Deterrence is achieved by hardening potential targets. The face of Washington, D.C., and most of the U.S. diplomatic missions around the world, has changed considerably in recent years. Barriers have been put into place to defend against car bombs, and access to many of these facilities is now tightly controlled. But as we harden one target category, such as government buildings, terrorists simply switch to a different set of targets, such as commercial office buildings. When these targets are hardened, they hit random targets, such as department stores and apartment buildings. Although it is impossible to achieve total deterrence through target hardening, we are forced to continue these efforts, especially when we are called upon to secure high-threat facilities.

Reaction to a terrorist event has been a focus of the U.S. government in both the military and law enforcement communities. Delta Force and the FBI's Hostage Rescue Team (HRT) are the most obvious examples of the United States commitment to develop a reaction capability. These units and the Navy SEALs are among the most respected and capable counterterrorism units in the world. Other well-known counterterrorism units include England's Special Air Service, the West German GSG-9, and the French Special Forces. Many other nations, from Holland to Kenya, also have excellent tactical response capabilities, and members from these countries often train with United States, British, West German, and French forces.

Prediction of terrorist activities and events is achieved through improved intelligence and counterintelligence capabilities. Within the United

States, the Federal Bureau of Investigation is responsible for these activities; outside of the country the U.S. agency with primary responsibility for intelligence and counterintelligence is the Central Intelligence Agency (CIA). Both of these organizations have developed terrorism intelligence specialists during the past decade and have significantly improved their capabilities in this area. From an international perspective, other nations have improved their proficiency in terrorism intelligence and counterintelligence, and many of these nations have developed systems for sharing valuable intelligence in an effort to combat this problem.

The official United States policy and response to terrorists are detailed in the *Public Report of the Vice President's Task Force on Combatting Terrorism.*[4] According to this report:

- The U.S. government is opposed to domestic and international terrorism and is prepared to act in concert with other nations or unilaterally when necessary to prevent or respond to terrorist acts.
- The U.S. government considers the practice of terrorism by any person or group a potential threat to its national security and will resist the use of terrorism by all legal means available.
- States that practice terrorism or actively support it will not do so without consequence. If there is evidence that a state is mounting or intends to conduct an act of terrorism against this country, the United States will take measures to protect its citizens, property, and interests.
- The U.S. government will make no concessions to terrorists. It will not pay ransoms, release prisoners, change its policies, or agree to other acts that might encourage additional terrorism. At the same time, the United States will use every available resource to gain the safe return of American citizens who are held hostage by terrorists.
- The United States will act in a strong manner against terrorists without surrendering basic freedoms or endangering democratic principles, and encourages other governments to take similar stands.

There are three levels of terrorism counteraction, as shown in Figure 2–1. The first level is the political/diplomatic level. The second level approaches the problem from a strategic perspective and involves the antiterrorism measures used to manage the threat. The third level is the

Figure 2-1
LEVELS OF TERRORISM COUNTERACTION

Level One – Political and Diplomatic Level

Negotiations

Changes in diplomatic relations

Sanctions

Military options

Level Two – Strategic Approaches

Threat analysis

—Intelligence collection

—Vulnerability surveys

Asset protection

—Operations security

—Personnel security

—Physical security

Level Three – Tactical Responses

Proactive operations

Reactive operations

—Tactical responses

—Hostage negotiations

—Retaliatory strikes

tactical level, and it includes both antiterrorism and counterterrorism activities.

LEVEL ONE—POLITICAL AND DIPLOMATIC

Level One includes two separate approaches to dealing with the problem of terrorism. The political approach addresses problems within a nation, that is, the methods used by a government to respond to the problem of domestic terrorism and, in some cases, international terrorism occurring within its boundaries. The diplomatic approach deals with communications and efforts between nations to address the problem.

Level One **political** approaches have ranged from total capitulation to extremely harsh measures. The harsh measures are sometimes openly sanctioned by the government, as, for example, when the British made carrying a lethal weapon on Cyprus a capital offense or when the government responds to acts of terrorism with extensive house-to-house searches. More covert examples of harsh government reactions are found in the death squads of Latin America. These government-sanctioned assassins have been responsible for the deaths of opposition leaders in numerous countries in Central and South America.

There are more moderate Level One political approaches being practiced. In some countries captured terrorists may be indicted under one set of charges that, if they are found guilty, will commit them to long prison terms without any possibility of parole. If they are charged under a different statute they will receive a much lighter sentence. Given a choice of which statute they will be charged under, many arrested group members have elected to cooperate with the authorities in exchange for the lighter sentence.

Another moderate approach is to invite the group to participate in the electoral process within the country. This is not really an effective approach because if terrorists could have achieved their objectives at the ballot box they wouldn't have become terrorists in the first place. In most cases, the terrorist infrastructure represents a small minority of the overall population. In Puerto Rico, for example, separatist groups want to create a socialist nation aligned with Cuba and the Soviet Union. But in all of the referendums held in Puerto Rico since the 1960s, the majority of the people have indicated that they prefer to either remain a commonwealth or become the fifty-first state. Less than 4 percent of the population wants to become a separate nation, and not all of these people aspire to create a socialist state. The Armed Forces of National Liberation (FALN), Los Macheteros, and the Organization of Volunteers for the Puerto Rican Revolution could never achieve their Cuban-supported objectives in an election.

In Colombia, former President Betencourt attempted to negotiate a truce with the major terrorist groups, inviting them to participate in the electoral process. The response of the Movement of April 19th (M-19) was a refusal to enter into negotiations, a closer alignment with the narcotics traffickers in the nation, and the assault on the Justice Palace in Bogota in November 1985. President Duarte offered the leftist groups in El Salvador the opportunity to put their desires to a vote; their response was to kidnap the president's daughter along with a number of Salvadoran officials. The terrorists' hostages were exchanged for 125 group members who were being held in Salvadoran jails.

Level One **diplomatic** approaches have ranged from diplomatic agreements to military attacks and all-out war. Remember that one of the incidents contributing to the start of World War I was the assassination of Austrian Archduke Franz Ferdinand by a Serbian terrorist trained by the Black Hand.

There have been a number of international agreements that were designed to help control terrorism. Many nations, for example, have agreed to return hijackers to the country from which the hijacked flight originated. But in reality Cuba has yet to return a hijacker to the United States, Iran was not about to return the Shiite hijackers who landed a Kuwaiti jet in Tehran in December 1984, and Western nations will not return an Eastern bloc hijacker who uses this tactic to escape to the West. However, there have also been international initiatives between Western nations that have resulted in improved cooperation in sharing intelligence and coordinating investigative activities. These coordinated efforts have prevented a number of incidents and have resulted in the arrest of some leading terrorists.

When state sponsors are identified, more drastic actions can be taken. Great Britain called for economic sanctions against Syria following repeated disclosures proving that the Syrian Embassy in London was used as a contact point for Abu Nidal terrorists operating in England. Although other nations were reluctant to participate in major sanctions against Syria, several European nations have required that country to reduce its diplomatic staff, thereby making it easier for the host country to monitor the activities of Syrian diplomats and at the same time making it more difficult for these ''diplomats'' to engage in subversive activities.

Another Level One alternative is to break off diplomatic relations with the countries sponsoring terrorism. The United States has done this with Libya and Iran, and Great Britain did also following the incident in which a British policewoman was killed by a shot fired from the Libyan Peoples Bureau in London. Although it may seem logical to break off all diplomatic relations in these cases, it actually creates a catch-22 situation. Nations communicate directly with each other through diplomatic channels. When there is a conflict or disagreement between nations, these channels become critical if we are to avoid misunderstandings, miscommunications, and an escalation of the conflict. To completely sever diplomatic relations with a nation prevents any possible direct diplomatic resolution of these conflicts and insures that these states will increase their use of terrorism as a covert means of warfare. An alternative approach would be to minimize the embassy staff of the offending nation to a single diplomat and a small secretarial staff. This would allow diplomatic channels to remain open but would make it almost impossible for the embassy to support subversive activities in the host country.

The most drastic Level One diplomatic response is military action. The Israeli government, for example, is known for its policy of striking back at the heart of the terrorist organizations operating against it. These retaliatory strikes have ranged from precision commando raids to major operations. The United States used this tactic following the bombing of La Belle discotheque in Berlin with the air strikes against Libya in April 1986. Although this option often appears to be justified, most of the nations in the world have repeatedly condemned military reprisals to terrorist actions.

Level One responses have had limited effectiveness in deterring terrorism or managing the overall problem. This is not surprising. As we have already discussed, there is no single underlying cause behind terrorism in the world today. Every major movement has its own set of motivating factors, and each situation must be dealt with according to the individual characteristics of that movement or group. The issues involved are extremely complex, and we are still attempting to find the most effective solutions to these problems.

LEVEL TWO—STRATEGIC APPROACHES

Most terrorism counteraction planners attempt to manage the problem at the second level using a number of strategic antiterrorism measures.

These activities begin with a threat analysis that includes the collection of information on groups operating in your area and a series of vulnerability surveys. Once the threat has been assessed and your vulnerabilities have been identified, you can develop asset protection approaches to manage the threat. It is important to remember that these are dynamic, rather than static, activities. The threat is constantly changing, and you must be prepared to monitor the changes as they occur and respond accordingly.

The group within your organization that is usually responsible for Level Two activities is the **threat management committee.** On a military installation or on a large defense contracting facility, this committee operates at the installation or facility level. In a municipal or law enforcement environment it operates at the department level. And in some private sector organizations the committee functions at the corporate level. The threat management committee is responsible for identifying the potential threat, developing antiterrorism programs to manage that threat, and coordinating or supporting the emergency operations center activities when an incident occurs.

Operations security is the cornerstone of an effective antiterrorism program. Terrorists must have the ability to predict your activities if they are going to develop an attack plan that insures a reasonable degree of success. To do this they need reliable information on your assets. Your operations security program will make it difficult for them to obtain the information they need, thereby significantly increasing the risks to the terrorist tactical cell.

Personnel and physical security are two additional components to your Level Two antiterrorism program. Personnel security begins with the correct level of awareness of the threat at all levels within the organization. It may also include security measures taken to protect high-threat individuals. Physical security programs are designed to keep the terrorists and their bombs out of the assets you are protecting by developing effective access control measures in combination with the other components of a comprehensive physical security program.

LEVEL THREE—TACTICAL RESPONSES

Most tactical responses to terrorism are proactive or counterterrorism measures. That is, they are initiated in response to a terrorist incident. These include the tactical team that goes into action during a hostage rescue mission, the hostage negotiation team that attempts to resolve the situation through negotiations, and the tactical team responsible for retaliatory actions that are sometimes taken after an incident. Counterterrorism measures also include the criminal investigation activities that take place after an incident occurs.

Tactical antiterrorism measures are also possible. These include military strikes against known terrorists and their training camps to disrupt the group's activities and to prevent them from attacking their targets.

Level Three also includes the activities that take place in the emergency operations center, or command center, when an incident occurs. Some of these activities and considerations will be discussed in Chapter Nine.

Referring again to Level Two, remember that when developing strategic and tactical responses to terrorism it is imperative that we first examine the threat against us. This includes the basic tactics used by terrorists and the current trends in the use of those tactics. Terrorism is a dynamic problem, one that is constantly changing. As the groups and the key players change, so do the tactics and the operational characteristics used by these adversaries.

KEY POINTS

1. Important definitions.
   a. Antiterrorism.
   b. Counterterrorism.
   c. Terrorism counteraction.
2. Terrorism counteraction mind-set.
   a. Overcome ethnocentric limitations.
   b. Think like a terrorist.
   c. Think like a terrorism counteraction planner.
   d. Expect the unexpected.
3. Terrorism counteraction objectives.
   a. Prevention.
   b. Deterrence.
   c. Reaction.
   d. Prediction.
4. Levels of terrorism counteraction.
   a. Political and diplomatic level.
   b. Strategic approaches.
   c. Tactical responses.

CHAPTER THREE

Terrorist Tactics

SCENARIO

"Look, Charlie, what I can tell you is that we think the group will become even more violent, and we think that may happen soon."

Dave Nelson was a thirteen-year veteran of the FBI. When the bureau assigned him to the Pleasantville office three years ago, he never thought he'd have to worry about terrorism in middle America. But all that had changed in the past few months. Dave had just returned from an FBI headquarters briefing on the Aryan Peoples Party, and he wanted to relay the seriousness of the threat to the local police department. He decided to give Deputy Chief Fox a call and was surprised when Fox asked him to come over right away. Apparently the police department was already concerned about the APP.

Nelson continued his briefing to Fox: "We know that APP group members have been responsible for several bombings, but in the past they would detonate the bombs in the middle of the night when there was little chance of casualties. However, the last two devices were planted in federal office buildings and they went off during lunch hour, when the APP knew there would be people in the halls. We've had three people killed and twenty-four injured just in those two bombings.

"The group also targets key adversaries for assassination. And we think they have at least ten people on their current hit list, including the Fort Richardson commander.

"That's the bad news," Nelson stated. "The good news is that there is no indication they are planning any hostage-taking events. Hostage-taking is just too expensive and too complicated for them at this time."

"OK, Dave, we know these guys are bad, and we know they have a compound twenty miles from where we're sitting. But will they really target Pleasantville?" Charlie Fox was hoping there was another reason for the group to locate near his city, but he couldn't think of a plausible explanation. Dave didn't answer directly, but went on with the briefing.

Both Fox and Nelson agreed that they needed to further analyze the threat from the APP before calling a meeting of the newly formed threat management committee. Nelson's FBI intelligence information was classified and could be shared only with Fox and Chief Casey. The rest of the threat management committee would have to deal with a generic threat statement unless the FBI believed that the community was in imminent danger. Then the classified information could be shared with all of the committee members.

The bureau was obtaining its information from an APP member who had "turned" but was still living at the compound. If the group learned the extent of the information that the FBI had, it would be obvious where it had come from, and their source would be killed. As always, the best way to keep information from leaking was to disseminate it strictly on a need-to-know basis.

"How about the potential for a megaterrorism act," Fox asked, "the possible use of a nuclear device or even a chemical or biological weapon?"

According to the information Nelson had received, the APP was considering the use of chemical agents. It was believed they had access to almost 170 pounds of cyanide that was originally the property of the Covenant, Sword, and the Arm of the Lord, an Arkansas-based group that the bureau had put out of business several years ago. The APP also had the ingredients needed to manufacture both mustard and nerve gas.

"But we don't think they can get a nuclear device." After his revelations about a potential chemical attack, Nelson acted as though this was good news. "There's only one free-lance group in the world that has the capability to make a terrorist-sized atomic bomb. They're located somewhere in the Mediterranean, and we don't believe they've been in contact with Pardue's people. Besides, they have plenty of potential customers with more money than the APP."

Dave Nelson was actually setting the stage. The FBI's major coup in turning the APP member was in learning that Jack Pardue maintained a journal of his thoughts and ideas. He thought of it as his own *Mein Kampf*. Since the FBI's source had access to that journal, they were now able to get inside Pardue's head and learn what makes him tick. They were also building a case that they hoped would put Pardue in prison for the rest of his life. Dave decided it was time to tell Fox what Pardue had planned for Pleasantville. He let Charlie read several recent entries from the journal.

The time has come for the Aryan Peoples Party to prove that we are not just another group of white supremacist radicals who lack the backbone needed to fulfill God's plan. Since arriving at this compound, I have reviewed a number of potential targets that have been surveilled by our intelligence cells. Now our job is to select the target that will bring ZOG to its knees and let the world know that Armageddon has begun.

Pleasantville is the ideal target. It represents all that is wrong with the Zionist Occupational Government. The town itself is a hotbed of race traitors and Zionist spies producing chemical and biological weapons that will eventually be turned against the white people of the United States when the Zionists and their Communist lackeys attempt to take complete control of the nation. The town deserves to be destroyed and all the agents of destruction needed to accomplish the mission are already here.

In addition, I have been able to recruit several members of the police department, two key personnel from the military installation, and a security guard at Toten Industries to our cause. These people remain in place as a covert action cell of the APP. Right now they are providing valuable intelligence information, but eventually they will be pulled together as a new tactical cell that will lead the action in Pleasantville.

Several potential targets are being considered. The main electric substation for the town is easy prey. A single explosive device could put the entire city in the dark for up to twelve hours. But there wouldn't be any casualties, and the movement needs casualties.

Another potential target is the Base School at Fort Richardson. Most of the students are children of the race traitors and foreigners who work there, and a good-sized bomb would guarantee a number of casualties. Better yet, the APP could release an anthrax agent that would kill all of the students and anyone else within several hundred yards, depending on which direction the wind was blowing. We already have the recipe and ingredients for the agent, and we've been waiting for the right opportunity to use them.

A third target being considered is the city hall and police station building. This would strike right at the heart of the local ZOG government. The plan is to send in a team of Aryan warriors that will kill everyone in sight with automatic weapons. The team would throw grenades into each room in the building and then head for the roof, where they think a helicopter will help them escape. Actually there will be no helicopter. By the time they reach the roof the police will have regrouped and will be reinforced by a unit from Fort Richardson. There is little hope that the tactical cell will actually escape, but that's part of the plan. The APP needs martyrs to inspire others to commit themselves totally to the cause.

One of our support cells is busy at work in a safe house located in Pleasantville constructing bombs that will be used for whatever purpose I eventually decide on. They are assembling the devices using portable radios and computers stuffed with plastic explosives. Any available space left in the bomb is filled with nails and other forms of shrapnel to increase its personnel killing capabilities. Our bomb builders were trained by members of the Popular

Front for the Liberation of Palestine–General Command during a visit to West Germany last year. We've promised to use this newly gained knowledge to bomb Israeli and Jewish targets in the United States.

I decided to send the bomb-building team to the safe house rather than bring them to the compound. Members living at the compound have identified a number of FBI agents and sheriff's deputies who are keeping the area under constant surveillance. In response, I've directed one of our intelligence cells to attempt to find a sympathetic supporter within the sheriff's department who can provide us with information on the department's capabilities and operations. I've also directed a separate team to develop a dossier on the sheriff and his family in case I decide to terminate or neutralize that threat.

The war against ZOG is about to begin, and Pleasantville will be the first major battle.

Charlie Fox had never felt so emotionally distraught in his life. He handed the copies of the journal pages back to Nelson and asked if the bureau had any idea who the two APP spies in the police department were. They did not. Somehow Charlie had to convey the seriousness of the threat to Chief Casey without being able to show him the journal, and to the mayor without letting him know that it even existed.

"I'll give you a call if we get anything else," said Nelson. "And let me know when you schedule the meeting of the threat management committee."

Nelson left, and Fox was alone with his thoughts. He knew he had to deal with the new level of the threat from the APP. He just wasn't sure how. Right now he didn't know whether he wanted to go for a long run or go home and have a drink.

Charlie reached for his workout bag.

*   *   *

Terrorists have at their disposal a variety of tactical options. They can bomb buildings or airliners, they can use rockets to attack police stations and embassies, they can assassinate diplomats, and they can take hostages or kidnap innocent victims. By comparison, groups that were operating a decade ago were not as lethal as the adversaries of today. Ten years ago bombs were detonated at night to cause damage but to minimize the possibility of casualties; targets selected for assassination were usually murdered while they were alone. Today's terrorists plant bombs at times and places designed to insure casualties, and when they commit an assassination they are prepared to kill not only the target but everyone around the target during their attack.

The basic tactics used by terrorist groups have evolved into a new level of lethality. This lethality is increased even further by the introduction of suicide terrorists and an increased potential for megaterrorism. Groups such as the Irish Republican Army (IRA) used to call in bomb threats before the devices went off so that police could clear the area. Now they take credit after the explosion has murdered and maimed. Religious fundamentalist groups such as the Shiites in the Middle East and the Christian Identity Movement extremists in the United States believe that God has ordained them to create the new world, and that any tactic used to achieve that goal, including murdering and maiming large numbers of people at one time, is justified. Terrorists in the world today believe that they are justified in murdering not only military and police personnel, but unarmed civilians including women and children. The mind-set of today's terrorist is illustrated in the old Russian anarchist saying that has recently been repeated by George Habash, the leader of the Popular Front for the Liberation of Palestine (PFLP): "There are no innocents!"

TRADITIONAL TACTICS

Bombs are the main tool of the terrorist! More than half of all terrorist incidents involve explosive devices and, as with other terrorist tactics, bombs are being used to kill more and more innocent people. There are several recent trends in the use of bombs by terrorists.

As we have already discussed, bombs are now being detonated so as to maximize casualties. Consider the massive car bombs that are detonated on a regular basis in Lebanon and in Ulster. It is not unusual for fifty or more people to be injured or killed in a single bombing, especially in Lebanon. The Red Army Faction's bomb at Rhein Mein Air Force Base in 1985 was detonated in a parking lot as people were arriving for work, and it was fortunate that more victims didn't die in the incident (two people were killed). To insure that they could gain entrance to Rhein Mein, the group kidnapped a serviceman the night before the bombing and murdered him for his identification.

Another trend in terrorist bombings is the use of secondary devices—

explosives that detonate some time after the initial bombs go off. Primary bombs are planted where they will maximize casualties. Then when the security forces and medical personnel respond to the incident, the secondary devices are detonated. The secondary bombs may be exploded using timers or radio detonators. This tactic was used when the Provisional IRA set off a series of bombs during the changing of the guard at Buckingham Palace. Another example of the use of secondary explosions involved an attack by the Basque separatist group Euskadi Ta Askatasuna (ETA) on a police station in Madrid in 1986. The ETA fired rockets at the police station from the backseat of a vehicle parked nearby. The rockets caused little damage and there were no initial casualties. However, when the police approached the vehicle after the attack, the car exploded, killing one of the officers.

The *Anarchist Cookbook,* a publication considered to be the terrorist bible during the 1960s and 1970s, includes a number of recipes for improvised explosive materials.[1] Terrorists during that period were making bombs out of ammonia-based fertilizer and petroleum products. These devices were unstable, however. In one incident, two members of the Weather Underground Organization died when their New York City bomb factory blew up as they were making bombs. Most terrorists today have moved beyond these homemade improvised explosive devices. They use construction explosives that can be easily stolen from construction sites all over the world, or they use military explosives that can be purchased on the international market or stolen from military installations. As a result, their bombs are much easier to conceal and are much more deadly. The bomb that was placed on Pan American Flight 103 was an unfortunate example of the latest technology available to terrorists and the increased lethality of their bombings. It is believed that the bomb was a Toshiba radio-cassette player packed with Semtex, a powerful Czech-made plastic explosive. This device, as small as it was, was enough to down a major aircraft and kill 270 people.

The increase in state-sponsored terrorism has resulted in more sophisticated terrorist bombs. The vehicle bomb detonated at the U.S. Marine Landing Team barracks at the Beirut airport on 23 October 1983 is a prime example of this new technology. The bomb consisted of 12,000 to 18,000 pounds of high explosive in a gas-enhanced configuration. This is accomplished by placing cylinders of volatile gas in the correct configuration with the explosive materials. The result is a detonation that is magnified far beyond the capacity of the explosive material itself. In fact, the Beirut bombing is estimated by the U.S. government to be the largest nonnuclear explosion in history.[2] It is believed that the bomb was designed and possibly manufactured in Iran.

Vehicle bombs can be extremely deadly because of the amount of explosive they can carry. Vehicle bombs are placed into one of five categories depending on the objective and nature of the bomb.

1. Vehicle bombs used to kill the occupants.
2. Vehicles used to deliver conventional bombs.
3. Vehicle-concealed launching systems such as the ETA rocket launcher previously discussed or the use of trucks by the Irish Republican Army to conceal and transport mortars, which then are fired from the bed of the truck.
4. Vehicles used to deliver massive and highly technical bombs like the one used at the Marine barracks.
5. Vehicles that are booby trapped.

Vehicles packed with large quantities of explosives are also being used to assassinate specific targets as the targets drive past the loaded vehicle. This tactic will be discussed in more detail in the section on assassination.

In recent years there appears to have been a decrease in the number of letter bombs used by terrorists. Since letter and package bombs are usually designed to maim rather than kill, this decrease is consistent with the trend to maximize casualties. However, these bombs are still being used by extremists around the world, so our antiterrorism training and other efforts must continue to address and counter this threat.

Arson is another tactic that has been a favorite of certain terrorist groups. Over the past twenty years, almost 14 percent of all terrorist incidents have been arsons, and in most cases an incendiary device was used to start the fire. The Ku Klux Klan and other white supremacist groups in the U.S. have burned a number of minority churches and synagogues as part of their subversive campaigns. Other groups around the world have repeatedly proven their proficiency in manufacturing and using Molotov cocktails.

European terrorists have developed a unique approach to the arson tactic. Before starting the fire they dress up as fire extinguisher service personnel and pick up all of the fire extinguishers in the target area, leaving behind extinguishers filled with flammable liquids along with a timer and an incendiary device. When the incendiary device ignites the fire, people in the immediate area attempt to put it out using the extinguishers that have been tampered with.

There appears to have been a decrease in the number of arsons committed by terrorists in the past couple of years. This could be the result of their increased access to construction and military explosives. And since potential victims of an arson may have the opportunity to escape during a fire, this decrease is also consistent with the trend to increase the number of casualties at each event.

Assassination was the earliest tactic used by terrorists. In fact, the word "assassin" is derived from the Hashshashin, or the Society of Assassins, the Islamic terrorists who operated in the Middle East during the tenth century. Diplomats and politicians have always been the favorite target of assassins, with military and police personnel coming in second. Today's terrorists, however, also assassinate business and cultural leaders, lower-ranking government and military personnel, and innocent civilians.

A new technique in using vehicle bombs has been applied during several assassinations in Europe. A large quantity of explosives is packed into a vehicle that is parked along a road where the target of the assassination is expected to travel. The bomb is usually wired for detonation by a terrorist hiding nearby. When the vehicle carrying the target approaches the bomb vehicle, the bomb is detonated and the shrapnel and the force of the explosion kill the target and anyone else riding in the vehicle with him. This tactic has been used by the Red Army Faction in West Germany and by Action Direct in France.

Assassinations also occur in retaliation for military actions against the terrorist group or its state sponsors. After the U.S. bombing of Libya in 1986, both British and American hostages were assassinated in Lebanon; Libya also offered up to $1 million each for additional U.S. hostages so that it could kill them. When the Israelis attack terrorist strongholds in Lebanon, the groups attacked sometimes retaliate by assassinating Lebanese Jewish citizens.

Assassination as a tactic allows the group to select a target for his or her symbolic value, for example, a diplomat from a certain country or an executive from a targeted company. This continues to be a favorite tactic of terrorist groups around the world.

Armed attacks by terrorists have become increasingly lethal in the past few years. Sikh terrorists in India have stopped bus loads of people on numerous occasions and murdered all of the Hindus on the buses by machine-gunning them to death. The victims usually include children, women, and older Hindus, who are indiscriminately slaughtered by their attackers. The same tactic is used by Tamil groups operating in Sri Lanka. In Peru the Shining Path (Sendaro Luminoso) has been responsible for more than 10,000 deaths in the past nine years.

Most armed attacks by terrorists are against unarmed civilians in an unprotected environment, such as an apartment building or a bus. Airports have also been targeted, for example, the Abu Nidal Group's attacks on the Rome and Vienna airports in December 1986 and the incident at Lod Airport in Israel in 1972. In all of those incidents the terrorists came to kill as many unarmed civilians as possible before they were killed or captured themselves.

Occasionally a terrorist cell will attack a military or police target. Sometimes the motivation is to get weapons and ammunition, but more often it is simply to demonstrate that they can successfully attack the "defenders of society." These attacks are most likely to occur in low-intensity conflict areas such as El Salvador, Lebanon, Sri Lanka, and the Philippines. Keep in mind, however, that the primary purpose of a terrorist attack is to terrorize, and more terror is created by murdering unarmed civilians including old people, women, children, and babies than by killing armed, or even unarmed, soldiers and police officers. Unfortunately we can expect the trend to continue of terrorists using armed attacks to kill large numbers of civilians.

Hostage-taking is an art that has been fine-tuned by international terrorists operating in the world today. They have learned to create spectacular events that are guaranteed to capture the attention of the media. When we examine the tactics being used during those events, several alarming trends emerge.

Most of today's hostage-taking events occur in a mobile environment. We no longer see the embassy takeovers of the 1970s. Instead, we find that hostage-taking and hijackings (or skyjackings) have been combined into a single tactic. By staying mobile, terrorists make it extremely difficult to plan and execute a tactical hostage rescue mission. While the tactical force is en route to one location, the terrorists simply move to another. Terrorists have learned that this approach allows them to control the dynamics and the media value of the event over an extended period of time.

While they are staying mobile, the hostage-takers monitor the world's response to the event, and they also listen for information on possible tactical responses being planned to end the incident. During the TWA

847 hijacking in 1985, the terrorists listened to newscasts about the event. At one point while they were on the ground in Algiers they learned that Delta Force was on its way to that location and they forced the pilot to fly to Beirut before Delta could arrive.[3] During the *Achille Lauro* incident, group members maintained radio contact with their leader, Abu el-Abbas, who provided them with information and instructions based on the world reaction to the incident and the objectives of the hijacking.

When possible, terrorists will move their mobile hostage-taking event to an airport that they or their cohorts control. When a Kuwaiti jet was seized by Shiite hijackers in December 1984, it was flown to Tehran, where the Iranian government orchestrated a theatrical rescue mission that supposedly saved the lives of the remaining passengers. The "rescue" took place after two Americans had been murdered and two others brutalized. The hijackers of TWA 847 landed in Beirut knowing that the airport was controlled, as much as any place is controlled in an anarchist environment, by the Amal Militia, a group sympathetic to their cause.

Perhaps the most alarming trend in terrorist hostage-taking events is that a victim is almost always killed during the early stages of the incident. On the Kuwaiti jet taken to Tehran, two U.S. State Department employees were shot. On TWA 847 a Navy diver was killed. An elderly man in a wheelchair was murdered on the *Achille Lauro*. But the most brutal example of this trend occurred on the Egyptian airliner hijacked to Malta in November of 1986.[4] The hijackers in that event decided to kill only Israeli and American women, and they shot five victims before Egyptian commandos stormed the aircraft. By killing a victim early in the event, the group members prove that they are committed to the action; it also increases the terror among the other victims still being held hostage.

A final trend that has occurred in terrorist hostage-taking events in the past few years is that the hostage-takers no longer negotiate with the authorities. On TWA 847, most of the demands were relayed through the captain of the aircraft. The same technique was used on the *Achille Lauro*.

We know from experience that at least three criteria must be established to insure a successful outcome in a hostage-taking event. First, we must have a tactical option available. By staying mobile and operating in friendly environments, terrorists have made this criterion hard to achieve. Next, the hostage-takers must have at least some desire to live. As we have already discussed, many terrorists are not only willing to die for their cause but some even have a desire to become martyrs. Finally, there must be communication and dialogue between the negotiator and the leader of the hostage-takers to either establish a rapport between these two people or to allow the negotiator to evaluate why that rapport cannot be established. By making all of their demands through one of their victims and then turning off the radio, terrorist hostage-takers deny us the opportunity for that communication. We can only conclude that terrorists have read the book on hostage-taking and are now one step ahead of us.

Kidnapping is an expensive event for a terrorist group unless they are operating in an environment like Beirut. To guard the victim and secure the area where he or she is being held requires a larger number of people than is usually found in a single tactical cell. And there is always the risk that the location will be identified by authorities.

This tactic was used extensively in the 1970s by Latin American groups that would kidnap victims for ransom. The largest ransom ever paid was $60 million, by a South American industrial family for the return of their two sons.[5] Today, however, these groups have a much more lucrative method for obtaining the funds they need—drug trafficking. Trafficking brings in more money and is much easier to maintain, so the incentive to kidnap victims for ransom has greatly diminished.

When terrorists do decide to kidnap a victim, the event is much more brutal than the kidnappings of a decade ago. When Aldo Moro, Christian Democratic statesman, was kidnapped by the Italian Red Brigade in 1978, all of his bodyguards were murdered. The event ended when Moro himself was killed. Even when the victims are returned safely, the terrorists usually come out the winner. In response to the 1987 "arms for hostages" deal between the U.S. and Iran, the group responsible for releasing the hostages in Lebanon responded by kidnapping two victims for each one released. They also tortured and murdered intelligence officer William Buckley, the primary hostage the U.S. wanted released.

Sabotage is an effective terrorist tactic against industrialized nations. Utility systems are one of the targets most frequently selected because they are extremely vulnerable and almost impossible to protect. More important is the fact that when they are hit correctly, a lot of people know it. Consider that one rifle bullet fired into a transformer at a substation at Montana's Flathead irrigation project caused 1,500 gallons of oil to leak from the transformer, destroying a $300,000 piece of equipment and resulting in a nine-hour blackout for a fifty-mile radius around the substation.[6]

Our increased reliance on information management and data processing systems is another major concern in combating terrorism. Such systems have been targeted on several occasions by European terrorists. The Internal Revenue Service has taken elaborate measures to protect its systems from attacks by antitax groups in the United States.

Threats can be an effective tool when used by an established terrorist group or its state sponsor. If a telephone caller in Ulster, claiming to be from the Irish Republican Army, says there is a bomb in a factory, that factory will probably be evacuated. Operations will be shut down temporarily even if no bomb is discovered.

To illustrate the potential impact of a threat or hoax, compute, if you can, the amount of effort and the cost expended by the U.S. government when it believed that Libya's Colonel Muammar Qaddafi had sent hit teams to the United States to assassinate President Reagan. The United States had to expend the effort even if Qaddafi had only started a rumor.

MEGATERRORISM TACTICS

The potential is very real for a megaterrorism incident in which thousands of people die. Terrorists have access to chemical and biological weapons, and it is conceivable that a state-sponsored or state-directed group could gain access to a nuclear device. In the past we discounted the possibility of a group committing this type of an event because of the backlash effect it would have on the group. The public becomes irate and demands action when several civilians are blown up on an airliner over Greece or when they are killed during an attack on the airport in Rome. But the public furor is usually short-lived. However, if an incident killed half of the people in San Francisco, the public outcry would continue until the terrorist group and the country sponsoring it were brought to justice.

This argument made sense in the past but it makes less sense today. Several of the most active terrorist movements in the world believe they are on a mission ordained by God and that any tactic used to achieve their goals is acceptable. This includes the use of megaterrorism. Would a nation like Iran that sent thousands of its teenagers to die in the world's most expensive war hesitate to kill a few thousand people it considers to be Satan worshipers?

We must remember that there are terrorists who actually desire to die for their cause. One such person drove the truck into the Marine Landing Team barracks in Beirut in 1983 and died along with his 241 victims.

Why should we expect a terrorist with the same mind-set to hesitate at releasing an agent from his car in Washington, D.C., that would kill everyone within a twenty-block radius? Megaterrorism is a major threat today, and we need to learn how to prevent and respond to the threat before an actual incident occurs. If we don't, there will be more than 241 victims.

Chemical and biological weapons present the greatest megaterrorism threat, and terrorist groups have already used some of these weapons on a small scale. The recipes and the ingredients needed to produce simple agents are readily available through a number of sources. In 1986 a Dutch scientist expressed concern that anyone with a basic knowledge of chemistry and $240 worth of materials could manufacture sixty pounds of mustard gas—enough to threaten a medium-sized city. Another scientist reported on the potential use of an anthrax agent. If this agent were dispersed as an aerosol compound into the air-conditioning system of a major building, it would kill everyone inside.

The current research and breakthroughs in bioengineering also present a new danger. Theoretically, it is possible to develop a specific strain that would kill only individuals of a targeted race. Imagine the horror we would face if today's theory becomes tomorrow's reality in the hands of a terrorist movement that believes in the superiority of the Aryan race.

Nuclear terrorism is also a threat. It is only a matter of time before state-sponsored or state-directed groups obtain nuclear devices that could be used anywhere in the world. It is possible that they could steal a nuclear weapon from a military stockpile, although these materials are well protected. There is also a remote possibility that a group could manufacture a nuclear bomb. However, due to the technology required and the tools and equipment that would be needed, this is not a major threat at this time.

TERRORIST TARGET SELECTION

Before we leave the discussion on tactics and move on to the specific responsibilities of a terrorism counteraction planner, we should examine the criteria used by the terrorist command cell and leaders to select targets. These criteria are based on interviews conducted by the media and law enforcement officials with a number of these people.[7]

1. Criticality of the target. What would the impact of an attack on the target be on the surrounding community?
2. Accessibility of the target. Can the tactical cell get to the target with a minimum of risk?
3. Recuperability of the target. How long will it take the target to get back to normal operations after the incident?
4. Vulnerability of the target. How difficult is it to disrupt or destroy the target?
5. Effect on the terrorist group. What will the public and government reaction be as a result of the incident?
6. Risk to the tactical cell. Will the terrorists committed to the attack be able to escape?

Notice that the effect on the group and the risk to the tactical cell are the last two criteria considered by the terrorist leaders. If they decide that the attack will achieve the publicity and other short-term objectives they desire, then they may commit to the attack plan regardless of the effect on the group or the safety of the tactical cell. This was demonstrated when Abu Nidal attacked the airports in Rome and Vienna. The world was appalled at the group's action, and most of the terrorists were killed. But it proved that the group is one of the most violent and committed in the world, and the attack generated the publicity and the notoriety that the leaders wanted.

We will discuss these criteria again in Chapter Five when we explore the various approaches and techniques used to develop an antiterrorism and a counterterrorism program.

KEY POINTS

1. Traditional tactics.
   a. Bombs—account for 50 percent of all incidents.
   b. Arson.
   c. Assassination.
   d. Armed attacks.
   e. Hostage-taking.
   f. Kidnapping.
   g. Sabotage.
   h. Threats.
2. Megaterrorism tactics.
   a. Chemical agents.
   b. Biological agents.
   c. Nuclear devices.
3. Terrorist target selection.
   a. Criticality of the target.
   b. Accessibility of the target.
   c. Recuperability of the target.
   d. Vulnerability of the target.
   e. Effect on the terrorist group.
   f. Risk to the tactical cell.

CHAPTER FOUR

The Threat Management Committee

SCENARIO

The plan was for the Pleasantville Police Department to serve as the sponsoring agency in the development of a community-wide threat management committee. The committee would develop contingency plans and agreements to address a number of potential threats, ranging from natural disasters to a major hazardous material incident at Toten Industries or Fort Richardson to a terrorist attack. Although Chief Casey would be the official chairperson of the committee, all of the organizations participating would have an equal voice, and each would be responsible for developing the specific threat assessment and response plans for its location and organization.

An hour before the initial meeting was to take place, Charlie Fox briefed Chief Casey on his conversation with Dave Nelson and the information they had discussed on Jack Pardue and the Aryan Peoples Party. As they walked down the hall to the conference room, the chief looked pensive and disturbed. The threat was worse than he had imagined.

Present at the first meeting were both Chief Casey and Charlie Fox; Dave Nelson; Lt. Col. Bob Marsh, the provost marshal at Fort Richardson; and John Filmore, a retired Air Force security officer now in charge of security for Toten Industries. Also present were Sara Lyndon of the Bureau of Alcohol, Tobacco, and Firearms, and Karen Dall, representing the State Emergency Management Agency. The group decided to invite several other agencies to participate on the Pleasantville Threat Management Committee, including the fire department and the state police. The initial tasks of the committee would include a listing of potential community-wide threats, the identification of sources of information on these threats, a list of vulnerable areas or targets, and the development of a specific threat statement. The committee members agreed that Charlie Fox would be the functional leader of the committee since Chief Casey was not expected to actually attend most of the meetings.

The group decided to divide up the responsibility for collecting relevant information from different sources. Fox would contact the National Technical Information Center and the National Institutes of Justice to locate data on the criminal threat from domestic terrorist groups. Lieutenant Colonel Marsh assumed responsibility for writing the Defense Technical Information Center. Dave Nelson would telephone the associations to which he belonged, including the American Society for Industrial Security and the Tactical Response Association.

Responsibility for various parts of the threat statement was given to members of the committee. Development of the terrorism threat statement was assigned to Dave Nelson and Sara Lyndon. It was understood that although their final product, that is, the terrorism threat statement, would be distributed only within the group, this statement was still limited to open-source and low-level classified information. These restrictions were based on each agency's individual requirements for the handling and sharing of classified information.

A community-wide crisis management team was also established by the threat management committee, with Chief Casey as the nominal chair of the group. The decision regarding who would actually take charge during an incident would depend on the nature of the incident itself. For example, if the situation involved a major law enforcement problem that was not under federal jurisdiction, such as a demonstration or hostage-taking incident, then Chief Casey would assume command of the crisis management team. If the event involved the release of chemical agents from Fort Richardson, then the base commander would assume control. And if the incident involved a terrorist attack, then the local special agent in charge of the FBI office, Dave Nelson's boss, would be in command, since, by federal law, the bureau is responsible for responding to and investigating all terrorist incidents within the United States.

Fox felt that the community-wide threat management committee should carefully delineate what responsibilities they would have and what responsibilities were left to the individual organizations. Once again the committee agreed that the development of the general threat statement and the formation of the crisis management team was a community-wide function. Antiterrorism measures including physical and personnel security would remain the responsibility of each company and agency. Each organization was also responsible for its operations and communications security.

Karen Dall suggested that the committee form a strong liaison with the chamber of commerce. In the event of a major disaster, heavy equipment could be needed to move broken concrete and rubble; since most businesses that own such equipment are chamber members, that organization is the logical point of contact. The committee took Karen's suggestion and also decided to identify other sources of equipment and specialized personnel.

Karen and John Filmore assumed responsibility for developing a list of contingency plans that the committee should prepare. Dave Nelson suggested they begin with plans to handle multiple bombings or an armed attack by a subversive group.

Legal questions also had to be addressed. Charlie Fox agreed to consult with the city's legal advisers regarding the proposed activities of the committee to make sure they weren't violating any laws or restrictions. Other members of the committee decided to check with their respective legal advisers as well.

Sara Lyndon suggested that the committee meet again in about four weeks but Fox and Nelson knew that they might not have that much time. They suggested that the committee meet for a special intelligence briefing the following week, and everyone agreed. Now it was up to Dave Nelson to figure out how he could convey the severe level of the current threat without revealing classified information.

The final topic discussed by the group was the need to develop scenarios that could be used for desktop exercises and full-blown field training exercises by the crisis management team. Charlie Fox suggested they consider a scenario involving an Aryan supremacy group led by a highly committed, sociopathic leader. Dave Nelson understood his motives.

After the meeting Fox asked Lieutenant Colonel Marsh if he had any information that would help him develop a set of vulnerability survey checklists for the police department. The Army had several different approaches to vulnerability assessments, according to Marsh: he promised to bring several different documents to the following week's intelligence briefing.

*   *   *

Most counterterrorism planners are familiar with the concept and operation of a crisis management team or an emergency operations center. This is the group that comes together when an incident occurs. It directs the tactical and logistical forces that are employed, provides liaison with other agencies or organizations, maintains the line of communication with both the incident area and higher headquarters or governmental offices, and makes or recommends decisions that can dramatically effect the outcome of the incident.

The crisis management team (CMT) is normally a reactive unit. Its role begins when a terrorist incident occurs. This unit can, however, adapt a proactive antiterrorism role that will contribute to the prevention of terrorism and increase the probability of effecting a positive outcome when and if an incident occurs.

In its proactive role, the CMT is referred to as the threat management committee (TMC). The committee may have the same basic members as the CMT, but its responsibilities are widely expanded. For purposes of this discussion, we will limit our focus to the counterterrorism responsibilities of the TMC, although the duties of the TMC and CMT may include other threats such as natural disasters and civil disorder.

Each member of the TMC has a specific area of expertise and responsibility. When an incident takes place and this group comes together as the CMT, it is important that each member assume his assigned role. In functioning as the TMC, however, there are several advantages to changing roles periodically. Everyone becomes aware of the overall functioning of the team; members do not become complacent in their accustomed roles and allow their level of performance to decline. And if the team comes together as a CMT, everyone will understand the responsibilities of the other members.

THREAT ASSESSMENT

One of the primary responsibilities of the TMC is to conduct periodic threat assessments. The threat assessment can be used to develop a specific statement that summarizes the threat to the installation, organization, geographic area, or personnel the TMC represents.

Most of the information needed to develop the threat assessment is available through open sources, such as newspapers, magazines, books, and special reports. Whenever an incident occurs, it is reported in the media. Magazines are constantly reporting on various group activities and the patterns of terrorism in all parts of the world. Professional researchers and special committees provide an abundance of reports on all aspects of terrorism.

All members of the TMC should be responsible for reading certain newspapers and magazines, abstracting information that could contribute to the threat assessment, and presenting their abstracts during TMC meetings. Specific publications are assigned to each member to avoid a duplication of effort. The same approach can be applied to books and reports on terrorism as they are published.

Special reports are available from a number of sources including the Defense Technical Information Service, National Technical Information Center, the U.S. Government Printing Office, and the Criminal Justice Information Service. Addresses for these sources are listed in Appendix B.

Although responsibility for the collection of general information is divided among the group members, the group member responsible for the intelligence function should also be responsible for developing and maintaining a data bank of terrorist incidents, provided this practice does not violate the regulations of the organization or any laws; many government and law enforcement agencies have explicit restrictions on the information they may collect and maintain on individuals and groups. Creating a data bank can be easily accomplished by entering the data on file cards or into a data-based management computer software system. The TMC that is responsible for a high-threat target or installation may decide to subscribe to a clipping service or to one of the specialized threat assessment publications or organizations, such as those listed in Appendix B, if the information is not available through other channels.

Other sources of information that can be used to develop threat assessment are intelligence collected by intelligence agencies and criminal information maintained by law enforcement agencies. This includes criminal information found in the FBI's National Crime Information Center (NCIC). This information is not generally provided to private organizations, and it is made available only on a need-to-know basis within the intelligence and law enforcement communities. The best way for the TMC to gain access to this information is to form a liaison with the appropriate agencies. These agencies will not be able to provide you with open access to their files, but they may provide you with input that is relevant to your threat statement. Remember, too, that they cannot provide you with classified information you are not authorized to receive, and that any information they do provide must be conveyed in a manner that is legal and within the procedural guidelines of the respective agency.

Now that you have this information, the big question is: so what?

Information by itself is nice to know, but a threat assessment and statement results from the synthesis of all available information.

Some of the questions you should ask when evaluating the information and developing your threat statement include:

- Are terrorists operating in our geographic area?
- Are terrorists attacking targets similar to the one we are protecting?
- What tactics are the terrorists using?
- Have there been indications of terrorist intelligence collection activities in our area?
- Are there subversive activities taking place in the area that could lead to terrorism?

The threat statement deals solely with the current and potential threat presented by your adversary. The assessment of your vulnerability to the threat and the measures you take to counter that vulnerability are addressed later and are not a part of the threat statement. The threat statement should be prepared by the person responsible for the intelligence function, approved by the threat management committee, and reviewed at least every three months by the TMC. If the activity you are protecting is in a high-threat area, such as a low-intensity conflict (LIC) area, or if the threat, for any other reason, is extremely dynamic, the statement should be reviewed at least once a month.

VULNERABILITY ASSESSMENT

Developing the threat statement is the first responsibility of the TMC. The next important activity is a vulnerability assessment. This involves all of the group members, and it should address four key areas:

- Operations Security
- Physical Security
- Personnel Security
- Communications Security

In order for a terrorist group to plan an attack on your activity, it must have the ability to assess your **operations security,** including the countermeasures you have developed. To identify and predict your operational patterns, the intelligence cell of a terrorist group may station their members across from your office, factory, or installation for several days. They will log each person's arrival and departure, and note shipping procedures, security guards' schedules, where people park, when doors and gates are open, and other key operational patterns. They will photograph these activities and your key employees, and they will record the names of vendors who are given access to your facilities.

The group will collect this information on several potential targets and then select the target that offers the greatest opportunity to plan and carry out a successful terrorist incident designed to help them accomplish their immediate objectives. If you make it difficult to collect this information, and even more difficult to predict your operations and countermeasures, your adversary may select an alternative target.

Since bombs continue to be the primary tool of the terrorist, the group may telephone a bomb threat to your organization in order to evaluate your response to those threats and see if you always evacuate the building when a threat is received. If you do have an evacuation plan, the surveillance team will want to learn where your personnel gather during the evacuation; this knowledge would help the terrorists maximize casualties. The group could telephone a bomb threat to your organization, wait until you evacuate, and then detonate the actual bombs in the evacuation areas.

Physical security is another important consideration when assessing your vulnerability. How easy is it to gain access, authorized or otherwise, to the facility you are protecting? Are fences or other barriers maintained? How secure are the doors and windows? Who has keys that access each area?

Many law enforcement agencies have crime prevention programs that can provide you with a physical security survey checklist. These checklists are also available in a number of security publications, books, and manuals.[1] These prepared checklists provide the basis from which the TMC should develop a physical security checklist designed specifically for your activity or facility. Start with several of the available survey forms and have one member integrate and modify them according to your needs. Next, have the entire committee review the survey and develop a final format. This format should be reviewed by the TMC annually or whenever major facility changes are made. More importantly, the survey should be conducted on a regular basis (at least once a year) to assess and identify your physical vulnerabilities.

If you have a large facility (that is, city, military installation, several industrial plants), you may decide to survey one building or facility each month. If you have a smaller facility located in a high-threat area, you may conduct the survey only every six months.

Responsibility for conducting the surveys should be rotated among team members, assigning one or two members to each survey. This way, conducting the survey does not become a routine (and potentially mundane) activity, and different "surveyors" will bring their own points of view to the assignment. Because one member will identify vulnerabilities that another may have overlooked, by rotating this responsibility you will make sure that all the bases are covered over a period of time.

A final suggestion on physical security. In general, team members should not conduct the physical security survey of the immediate area where they work, although they should accompany the survey team and point out weaknesses that they are aware of. All human beings have a tendency to adapt to their immediate surroundings, and it may be difficult for a team member to survey his area with a fresh perspective and to identify problems he has long since taken for granted.

Evaluating your vulnerability in the area of **personnel security** may not be difficult, but countering the threat in this area could be one of your most challenging terrorism counteraction responsibilities. This threat is evaluated from two perspectives.

First, who are the individuals who would be the most attractive targets to a terrorist group, and why? Since the objective of most terrorist incidents is publicity, well-known individuals or persons in well-known roles are at risk. Picasso is thought to have appeared on a number of terrorist hit lists, not because he was a political figure but because an attack on him guaranteed worldwide publicity. On the other hand, how many people had heard of Brigadier General James Dozier before he was kidnapped by the Brigate Rosse? He became a target because of the role he occupied as a key NATO military official.

The other perspective to consider in determining your personnel security vulnerability is who has access to what. You need to know your personnel, what information they have access to, and what each person's attitude is toward security.

Terrorists collect intelligence information from employees at the facilities they target. An employee may talk too much to someone they just met at a bar, or an employee may be sympathetic to the subversive cause and knowingly provide information to your adversary as a member of the passive support structure. Your facility or organization may even be in-filtrated by terrorists or their active supporters.

If you are going to effectively counter these threats, your personnel must first believe that the threats exist and then must be willing to help you manage them. Unfortunately, in some cases, people who could be primary targets of a terrorist action are unwilling to accept the reality of the threat or to accept personal responsibility for helping to respond to it. As an example, Brigadier General Dozier was informed that he had possibly been targeted for kidnapping, but he chose to ignore the threat and the recommendations that would have improved his security posture. He continued to live in a civilian setting instead of accepting the added security of installation quarters, and he opened the door of his apartment to a group of bogus plumbers who were actually his Brigate Rosse ab-ductors.[2]

Several years ago the Turkish counsel general in Los Angeles refused to allow professional bodyguards to accompany him to and from his home, even after an attempted firebombing of his house and in spite of a threat issued by an Armenian terrorist organization. One day while driving to work he was assassinated by two terrorists when he stopped at a traffic light.

In most cases you cannot afford to assign a twenty-four-hour bodyguard detail to all high-risk targets. The target must be willing to accept primary responsibility for his own protection. He must be alert to unusual persons or activities around the office or the house. He should vary his routes and times between the home, office, and other locations. He must insure that his residence is secure and that he does not open the door without knowing who is on the other side, and make sure his family and employees know they should report unusual people or occurrences, and to whom they should report these situations.

When a key individual is considered a high risk, then bodyguards, or personal security details, may be necessary. Obviously you need to know something about the people you are using as bodyguards, including the qualifications and background of each of these individuals. Also, make sure the principal (the person being protected) understands the duties of the bodyguards and how to cooperate with them as they perform these duties.

As difficult as it is for some high-risk principals to understand and accept the risk, it is even more difficult for other employees and individuals to understand their roles in providing for personnel security. In high-risk situations such as diplomatic missions, defense-related factories and in-stallations, and corporate headquarters, every employee should be screened before being hired or assigned to the facility. Check each employee's background so you know who you are hiring, even for the most basic jobs. A janitor who can't read still can be bribed and asked to deliver the trash from the corporate boardroom to a terrorist intelligence unit. This trash may provide your adversary with all the information needed to plan a successful attack. The same janitor could also plant a bug (transmitter) in a sensitive area of the facility, if the price is right.

Knowing who you hire is just the first step to dealing with this threat. You must also assess the security awareness and attitude of the people who have access to your information and operations. Some people will never accept the reality of the threat and therefore should not have access to even basic operational plans or other information. They are likely to compromise that information unknowingly as a result of their naiveté.

When determining your personnel security vulnerability, some of the questions you should ask are:

- Who are the high-risk individuals associated with this activity?
- Are these individuals willing to accept primary responsibility for their personal security?
- Is the risk great enough to justify employing bodyguards or a personal security detail?
- Are we limiting access to information and operational patterns on a need-to-know basis with all employees?
- Do we require a background investigation or other screening of all personnel who have access to operational plans or other sensitive information?
- What are the awareness and attitudes of our employees regarding security?
- Do we reevaluate these attitudes on a regular basis (for example, once a year)?
- Have we also evaluated the background and attitudes of the vendors we work with and the other outsiders who have access to infor-mation on our facility?
- Do we have highly restrictive measures that limit the information vendors and other outsiders can obtain regarding our facility and our activities?

A final area of vulnerability that the TMC should evaluate and monitor is **communications security.** Modern technology has made the interception of telephonic messages and the use of covert listening devices extremely easy and inexpensive.[3] The bug your adversary could use to monitor your office conversations might cost less than $15. The equipment used to detect it could cost thousands of dollars. And once it was detected you would probably never be able to prove who had planted it, or learn what or how much information was compromised before the transmitter was discovered. Your telephone lines could be tapped at a point beyond your own office and never be detected. It's even possible to monitor thousands of telephone conversations within a given geographic area and record only a preselected few.

In high-risk situations you need to purchase sophisticated countersurveillance equipment and train security employees to use it, or else contract with a professional firm to conduct these activities. If you do contract for countersurveillance work, be sure you know whom you hire. Check their references and discuss their qualifications with local and federal law enforcement agencies. Some of the firms you hire to sweep the office may actually be *planting* listening devices.

Scramblers can also be useful if you have a high-risk activity. These devices make it difficult for someone intercepting a telephone transmission to know what you are discussing. Remember, however, that if a transmitter is planted in a room where one of the people on the telephone is located, the effectiveness of the scrambler is almost neutralized.

Terrorists of the not-so-distant future may also target your computers to gather information. They are already targeting computer centers for attacks, and many of the states that sponsor terrorist groups have the capability to covertly tap into the information stored or being entered into your data processing equipment.

Assessing your vulnerabilities is a dynamic activity. It never ends. At each meeting of the threat management committee, you should review the vulnerabilities that have been identified since the last meeting and discuss appropriate countermeasures to address each of the identified vulnerable areas. The TMC should then assign responsibilities to the appropriate team members for additional vulnerability assessments and physical security surveys to be conducted prior to the next meeting. The results of those assessments and surveys will be presented at the next committee meeting.

LIAISON WITH OTHER ORGANIZATIONS

Establishing and maintaining liaisons with other organizations is another responsibility of the TMC. The type of organizations included in these liaisons depends on the threat to your activity, the type of activity you represent, and the availability of specific support agencies.

Law enforcement and military units should be high on your list. Local law enforcement agencies in the United States should establish an association with the FBI. Private sector organizations may need to establish a liaison with both local and federal law enforcement agencies. And all law enforcement agencies should have an established liaison with any military activities in their area (and vice versa).

Relationships among and with other agencies must be governed by applicable laws and agency guidelines. For example, in the U.S. under the Posse Comitatus Act, military units may not be used in tactical activities in support of civilian law enforcement without the approval of the president or his authorized representative. The military may, however, provide logistical support and equipment, and military personnel to maintain that equipment.

If your threat statement includes the possibility of a major bombing, you will also need to establish a liaison with a medical facility and demolition personnel if these are not available within your organization. In developing your contingency plans you may find that the only adequate medical facility is some distance away. In that case, you will need to establish a liaison with an aviation activity to transport potential victims.

Most law enforcement agencies, military facilities, and defense industries with tactical units (for example, SWAT [Special Weapons and Tactics], EST [Emergency Specialist Teams], or SRT [Special Response Teams]) also have cooperative agreements or memorandums of agreement with other similar activities and organizations. If a situation requires a greater tactical response than you are capable of providing, these other units can augment your forces.

Review your threat statement and determine what assets would be required if the worst possible scenario were to occur. Then inventory the assets you have readily available. Begin planning your liaisons by contacting the required law enforcement agencies, such as the local police and the FBI, and then expand this activity by contacting other organizations that can help to fill the gaps between the worst possible scenario threat and the assets you have available to respond to that threat.

CONTINGENCY PLANNING AND TRAINING

At this point the threat management committee has identified the threat and your vulnerabilities. Now you are ready to begin developing your team.

The TMC should discuss in depth the need for contingency plan development. Using the threat statement, list the possible scenarios you could be confronted with and then list the stereotype responses you would use if those scenarios occurred. Next, list the different contingency plans you need to develop to detail your activities in response to each scenario. Now assign responsibility for preparing drafts of these contingency plans to individual team members.[4]

The initial draft and the final plans should be kept as simple as possible. List who is to be notified and in what order, outline the assets you will use for your initial response, and determine which organizations should be contacted if an incident were to occur. After the draft contingency plans have been prepared by individual members of the group, they should be reviewed and finalized by the entire TMC.

To test the effectiveness of your plans, and to test the team's ability to respond as the CMT, use these scenarios to plan and conduct CMT training exercises. Ask an outside agency such as a law enforcement tactical team or a security consulting firm to help plan a command post exercise (CPX) or desktop exercise based on your scenarios. During the exercise your team should have to respond to an ongoing crisis situation as if they were actually performing their functions as the CMT.

Every year or so, plan a major training exercise that includes your tactical unit (if you have one) and your liaison organizations. To make this field training exercise (FTX) realistic, ask another tactical team to assume the role of the aggressor and act out the part of your adversary as it is detailed in your threat statement.

The CPX or FTX should last at least three to four hours. An all-day exercise is even better, and a three- or four-day exercise is superb (although very few organizations will commit to such extensive training). Immediately following the training you should conduct a debriefing and discuss the actions of all the players at each point in the exercise and the lessons learned. The debriefing should be documented for future review and evaluation by the team.

A word of caution. A terrorist intelligence unit would love to observe and photograph this training. They could identify all of your counterterrorism (CT) personnel, assess your CT capabilities, and identify your most vulnerable weaknesses. Security regarding, and during, these exercises is mandatory. As part of this security, have countersurveillance personnel watch for curious onlookers and for aircraft flying over the training area. You should photograph these people, the vehicles they are driving, and the aircraft they are flying. Record all identifying numbers, including license tags and aircraft or boat registration numbers. Also be alert for suspicious radio communications in the area. You may consider taking your counterintelligence photos openly, so anyone collecting information will know they can be identified.

When engaged in countersurveillance activities, don't ignore anyone. The beautiful family with the cute little children may be your most dangerous adversary. The little old lady in the old Ford may have a camera hidden in her bag. It wouldn't be the first time!

AWARENESS FUNCTION

Another responsibility of the TMC members is the "awareness function." Each member should be constantly aware of the new "mayhem manuals," terrorist-related publications, and terrorism counteraction publications as they become available.

There are more than 2,000 mayhem manuals available on bookshelves and through mail-order publishers. Many of these are military manuals reprinted for public use. These publications describe in detail how to make explosive bombs and incendiary devices, build silencers, assassinate a target, bug a facility, and detect bugs at the terrorist safe house. Some of these manuals include formulas for agents such as nerve gas and mustard gas.

Terrorists and their support groups often publish their own newspapers, magazines, or pamphlets. One antiutility group printed a publication that included propaganda on how the utility was "screwing" its consumers, information on how to build bombs, and photographs and home addresses of the board of directors of the utility.[5] As with many underground publications, their information was not up to date. After the publication was distributed, someone ringed firebombs around the reported residence of one of the utility's directors. The director had moved six months earlier, however, and the new resident, whose house was damaged, had no connection with the utility company.

As new terrorism counteraction publications become available, they should be reviewed by the TMC for new and useful ideas. Individual TMC members should be assigned responsibility for each publication. The member could then prepare a report on the publication, including recommendations for the TMC to consider.

PREVENTING A TERRORIST ATTACK

There are four points in the preparation for, and in the initial stages of, an attack at which terrorists are most vulnerable. If you develop countermeasures that take advantage of these vulnerabilities, you can decrease the probability of a successful attack against your activity or facility.

The first is during **the intelligence-gathering phase.** Terrorist groups must have intelligence information to plan an attack. If you deny them this intelligence, using the approaches already discussed and the operations security (OPSEC) procedures discussed in Chapter Six, it becomes more difficult for them to plan an attack against you. Keep in mind, however, that some facilities are such attractive targets that terrorists may select them even though the group has not been able to collect the intelligence information they would like to acquire.

The second point at which terrorists are most vulnerable is during their **movement to the target** or target area. International terrorists in particular seldom travel from their initial departure point to the target carrying their weapons, explosives, or other supplies or equipment. Support cells or active supporters furnish these materials at strategic points en route. Disrupting the travel itinerary of the attack cell or their supporters has prevented incidents from occurring. Controlling access to facilities you are protecting can also help you to accomplish this objective.

The next point of vulnerability is during the **initial attack.** Terrorists use diversionary tactics to pull security forces away from the primary target. Bombs may be detonated miles from the target so that police, fire, and medical personnel are responding to those explosions while the terrorists detonate devices at the primary target or while they kidnap their intended victim. If your security or law enforcement personnel have secured their assigned areas rather than responding to the diversionary tactic, the terrorists may find that the primary target is still protected and they will not be able to carry out their original plan.

Another example of the vulnerability of terrorists during the initial attack stage was demonstrated during the Dozier incident. The Brigate Rosse terrorists knocked on Brigadier General Dozier's door saying that they were plumbers who needed to check on a reported leak. Had they been challenged before the door was opened, they may have had difficulty gaining access to the apartment before the police arrived.

The fourth point of vulnerability is **predicting your counterterrorism response.** For more than a decade, South American terrorists kidnapped American business executives because they knew that the executive's company would pay a ransom for their release. When some of the target companies refused to pay a ransom, the outcome was less predictable and the rate of kidnappings decreased. (And, as we've already discussed, these groups have found that narcotics trafficking is a much easier and more reliable method of financing their causes.)

Your adversary must also predict your tactical response capabilities and plans. If you have a SWAT or an SRT, they need to know how well this unit is trained and what its capabilities are. This is why it is imperative that the threat management committee protect all contingency plans and be alert to potential intelligence-gathering activities during training exercises.

Be sure to consider each of these areas of vulnerability when you are conducting TMC activities and preparing your contingency plans. Try to take advantage of these areas. If you are successful, you may convince the group to attack an alternative target, or you may stop an attack during its initial stages.

TMC ORGANIZATION

Now for the most difficult questions: Who should be on the TMC and what should each member's role and responsibilities include? The problem in addressing this question is that the answer depends on the setting (for example, civilian, law enforcement, military, political), the type of activity you are protecting, and the assets and personnel from which you are selecting team members. Because each of these variables must be considered, we will discuss the organization of the team in generic terms, identifying each function or role and letting you decide who should fill that role.

Ideally the team should consist of five to nine members, since research indicates that this is the best size for any crisis decision-making group. The role of each team member for an eight-person TMC would be defined as:

1. TMC Leader
2. Assistant Leader/Recorder
3. Personnel Specialist
4. Intelligence Specialist
5. Logistics Specialist
6. Operations Specialist
7. Legal Adviser
8. Public Affairs/Information Specialist

Every committee or team needs a **leader.** Selecting the person to fill this role isn't always as easy as it sounds. The leader of the TMC should be the same person who will manage the crisis management team if an incident actually occurs. In the military this may be the installation commander. The chief executive officer (CEO) of a company may want to manage the crisis if a private sector organization is involved, and in the public sector it may be the governor, mayor, or police chief.

The primary problem you will face in selecting the leader is that these key people seldom have the time to participate in the TMC's activities or to attend all of the meetings or training exercises. But when an incident occurs and you are confronted with a real crisis situation (and the media cameras are rolling), they will want to take charge.

A secondary problem is that this key person may be the target of the attack. If the mayor does commit to leading the CMT and participating in all of the training, what happens when an actual hostage situation occurs with the mayor and his family as the victims?

The **assistant leader/recorder** fills two important roles. First, this person takes command of the group if the leader is not present. When the leader is present this person maintains a log of all major happenings, including the activities of the terrorists, the CMT, and the supporting activities or forces, and assists in managing the emergency operations center. The log is maintained to develop after-action reports and lessons learned reports, and to support the team's activities if the incident results in post-incident litigation. Every terrorist incident is a crime and a potential source of criminal and civil litigation (lawsuits). The log and other records maintained by the assistant leader will prove to be extremely important documents if the incident results in judicial proceedings.

The **personnel specialist** will have identified the tactical and support personnel required to respond to the potential scenarios and contingency plans developed by the TMC. This team member is also responsible for establishing liaisons with other organizations that will help augment your available forces if they are needed. During an incident this person maintains a record of the personnel currently committed, personnel available for augmentation or reinforcement, and potential personnel needs that may emerge as the incident evolves.

The **intelligence specialist** is the conduit through which intelligence information is channeled into the CMT when an incident takes place. Some of the functions of this role while the team is in its TMC posture have already been discussed. They include the development of the threat statement and participation in the preparation of the scenarios for the command post and field training exercises.

The **logistics specialist** plans for all of the logistical support that will be needed if the contingency plans are activated, and he also coordinates these activities when they are actually needed. This member keeps track of the supplies and equipment already committed to the situation, plans for the materials that will be required as the incident continues, and attempts to plan for other logistical needs that may be required depending on how the incident unfolds. During the proactive TMC stage, he initiates liaisons with potential sources for this logistical support and maintains inventory records.

One of the key roles on the team is the **operations specialist.** This person has a thorough knowledge of the organization's tactical support capabilities and the options outlined in the contingency plans. He helps to identify potential personnel and logistical needs, and he works with the TMC members responsible for these areas. When the CMT is activated, he becomes one of the team leader's most important advisers.

Because every terrorist incident is a legal event, your team should include an attorney as its **legal adviser.** Potential legal consequences should not be the deciding factor as the team makes decisions, but they are important considerations. The input from this team member will help to insure that your contingency plans are developed, and that your TMC activities are conducted within the appropriate legal framework. When the CMT is activated, this member will help you avoid, and respond to, post-incident litigation.

Every terrorist event is a media event, so every threat management committee and crisis management team must have a **public information specialist** (public affairs officer). This person is prepared to handle the unique demands of working with the media during an ongoing terrorist event.

Eight people cannot prepare for or manage a terrorist incident by themselves. They need a viable support structure. The elements and responsibilities of this support structure depend on all of the variables considered when deciding the organization of the threat management committee and crisis management team. Your TMC will identify the specific positions to be included in your plan and the organizational structure of the team and its support functions as one of its early activities.

Don't select team members solely on the basis of their position and qualifications. Consider also their awareness of the terrorist threat and their personal commitment and interest in responding to it. Team members who resent having to spend time on the committee, or who refuse to acknowledge that the terrorist threat exists, will be a detriment to the team and its activities. Try to select members who perform well under pressure, are willing to share in (rather than dominate) team decisions, and offer the needed expertise in their specialty area.

At the first meeting of the team, list all of the group's responsibilities and related tasks and prioritize them. Then assign tasks to team members on the basis of the priority of those tasks and the expertise and interests of the team members. Unless the threat is imminent, don't try to complete all the tasks immediately or you'll burn out your team members. Establish a one- to three-year plan and decide how often the team will meet (for example, monthly or quarterly) to evaluate its progress.

Once the TMC is functioning, your antiterrorism program is operational. And as a result of having an effective antiterrorism program, you may convince the terrorist group leaders to select an alternative target. In the event that you are targeted, you will be better prepared to respond to the incident and contribute to a positive outcome.

IMPLEMENTATION CHECKLIST

1. Decide who will be on the threat management committee. Be sure that all of the roles listed at the end of this checklist are included.
2. Conduct the threat assessment.
   a. Assign responsibility for monitoring open-source publications to TMC members.
   b. Have your intelligence TMC member prepare an incident data base or file. A file on each group that represents a threat to your assets should also be developed.
   c. Use the information you've collected to prepare a threat statement.
3. Conduct your vulnerability surveys. Consider each of the following areas:
   a. Operations security.
   b. Physical security.
   c. Personnel security.
   d. Communications security.
4. Establish liaisons with other organizations.
   a. Local and federal law enforcement agencies.
   b. Medical facilities.
   c. Other activities according to your threat statement.
5. Contingency planning and training.
   a. Develop a series of possible scenarios.
   b. Prepare contingency plans to respond to these scenarios.
   c. Test your plans using desktop exercises.
   d. Test your plans using field training exercises.
   e. Maintain countersurveillance during all training.
6. Awareness function.
   a. Monitor all appropriate counterculture publications.
   b. Review all new terrorism counteraction publications.
7. Consider all terrorist vulnerability points when developing your programs.
   a. Intelligence collection.
   b. Movement to the target.
   c. Initial attack.
   d. Predicting your counterterrorism response.
8. Make sure that each of the eight generic roles are assigned to members of the threat management committee and the crisis management team.

a. Team leader.
b. Assistant leader/recorder.
c. Personnel specialist.
d. Intelligence specialist.
e. Logistics specialist.
f. Operations specialist.
g. Legal adviser.
h. Public affairs/information specialist.

CHAPTER FIVE

Threat Analysis

SCENARIO

"That's about it. We know that the Aryan Peoples Party is planning some kind of action in Pleasantville. We also know that the Committee Against Chemical Warfare may be planning to establish a local chapter, which could mean they're planning a series of demonstrations here." Dave Nelson was completing his intelligence briefing for the threat management committee. He had summarized the FBI data on the two groups without revealing his sources or identifying the information they had obtained from Jack Pardue's journal.

"It should be obvious that this committee has two immediate tasks," he continued. "First, we need to get an antiterrorism plan into effect quickly. And second, we need to stay on top of the information on these two groups as it becomes available."

"Do we need to set up a local data base to track the members of the group and their actions?" The question came from Karen Dall, the State Emergency Management Agency representative.

"The bureau already has that capability, and while most of our information is classified, I think we can get special permission to release all relevant data to this group."

Charlie Fox jumped in. "There's also a question on the legality of a public ad hoc committee maintaining files on individuals and groups. Rather than duplicate the effort and maybe get ourselves into hot water, I suggest we go along with Dave."

Everyone agreed.

Lieutenant Colonel Marsh had prepared a modified list of local threat indicators, based on research conducted at the Army Intelligence School.

The list included items such as reports of stolen firearms and increased activism around specific causes. He had attempted to localize the list to fit the needs of this committee, and after several other adjustments were suggested, it was agreed that Marsh would be responsible for maintaining this activity. The threat indicator list would be programmed into a computer at Fort Richardson. Bob Marsh would then have an update of the indicators prepared before each month's meeting so the committee would have some objective data to help them determine if the threat level was increasing or decreasing.

Marsh also had brought a set of vulnerability-determination systems developed by the Army. The committee decided that each of the agencies and companies present would be responsible for modifying these materials for use within their own organizations. The threat management committee would be responsible for maintaining the intelligence and threat indicator list, but each organization was responsible for the security of its assets.

Pleasantville now had a functioning threat management committee. Responsibilities had been assigned and duties had been assumed. In light of the information learned during today's intelligence briefing, the committee agreed to meet again the following week to discuss the drafts of the contingency plans developed by various committee members and to organize a series of desktop and field exercises to test these terrorism counteraction plans.

Unfortunately, the committee and the plans they were working on would be tested sooner than they had imagined.

At the Aryan Peoples Party compound, Jack Pardue was reviewing his intelligence collection activities. He was receiving a constant flow of information from his active supporters at the police department and Toten Industries, and he had identified several passive supporters at the sheriff's department. These people were being encouraged to provide the APP with information that would "help the cause."

His access to open-source information had proved to be invaluable. An accomplice had used the Freedom of Information Act to obtain the floor plans for all the buildings at Fort Richardson, and another group member had purchased satellite photos of the fort and of Toten Industries. Jack knew the location of every building and every fence at and around those facilities. Another member had visited the local newspaper and had done a background search of information on Sheriff Potter. He provided Jack with information on the sheriff's entire career, his family, and his house. The Living Section of the newspaper had featured the sheriff's home just eight months ago, and the APP now had pictures of every room plus a floor plan.

Jack had learned that a threat management committee had been formed, with the FBI taking an active role. To make sure he wasn't caught off guard, he had an active supporter who worked for the city maintenance department plant a listening device in the police department conference room. The "bug" was attached to a voice-activated tape recorder located in the basement maintenance room in the building. After listening to the tapes of the committee's intelligence briefing, Jack decided to move up the timetable on his plan of action.

The police department was also under surveillance, and the APP intelligence cell had instructions to photograph people entering and leaving the building before and after the threat management committee meetings. He wanted to know exactly what his ZOG adversaries looked like. He wondered what they would look like through the scope of a high-power sniper rifle.

* * *

Step back for a moment and take an objective look at the assets you are responsible for protecting. If you were a terrorist who wanted to attack or disrupt these assets, how would you accomplish that objective? The first step to an effective threat analysis is to learn to think like a terrorist. You have to understand the mind-set, the motivation, the capabilities, and the short- and long-range goals of each of the groups operating in your area.

Not all of the groups active in your area may pose a direct threat to you. Right-wing, neo-Nazi groups in the United States, for example, target government and military facilities because they consider themselves at war with ZOG, and banks and armored cars because they need money to fund their activities. These groups do not necessarily present a threat to an industrial target unless that facility is associated with or supports a U.S. government asset.

By now you have begun to develop information on your adversaries, and you have also conducted a vulnerability study of your facilities. Conducting the threat assessment and the vulnerability surveys is a continuous process, since the composition and capabilities of terrorist groups are constantly changing and because your security posture will change over time. Because this is a dynamic process, you will be periodically validating your threat assessment and vulnerabilities through the use of scenario development, "war gaming," and a periodic review and consultation conducted by personnel from outside the immediate environment.

CURRENT TERRORIST TRENDS

Monitoring current terrorist trends is not as difficult as it may sound. Whereas professional intelligence agencies such as the Central Intelligence Agency and the Federal Bureau of Investigation collect and analyze large amounts of classified and unclassified information, private corporations and others concerned with protecting local assets can also collect and analyze current information on terrorist groups and trends, largely through the use of open-source information (see Appendix B).

Begin your threat analysis by identifying your geographic areas of interest and the types of targets that concern you. Even with today's international travel and communications capabilities, most groups limit their operations to a well-defined geographic area and/or category of targets. In Europe, for example, the Red Army Faction is active in West Germany and the Brigate Rosse in Italy, and the Action Direct was active only in France. In the United States the New World Liberation Front confined its activities to the West Coast; the United Freedom Front operated primarily in the Northeast; and most of the Puerto Rican separatist groups' activities have been limited to New York, Chicago, and Puerto Rico, with the exception of the West Hartford armored car robbery in September 1983 that netted $7.2 million for Los Macheteros. Most of the groups that do operate nationally or internationally repeatedly attack certain categories of targets. Armenian terrorists have been active in the Middle East, Europe, and North America, but most of their targets have been Turkish diplomats and other Turkish interests. Most Palestinian terrorism is directed against Israeli or Jewish targets, although they also engage in random actions against other targets, primarily Western nations that support Israel.

The next step is to define the information you will collect and maintain, the sources of that information, and the people who will be responsible for these activities. It will be to your advantage to develop a computer-based system using any of the data-based management software packages available. The basic unit of analysis for most terrorist information management systems, whether you are storing your data on computer disks or using file cards, is the terrorist incident. Whenever a bomb explodes, an assassination occurs, or any other terrorist event takes place in your geographic and target-category areas of interest, that incident becomes a record in your data-based system. The basic fields (units of information) in most systems include:

- Date of the incident.
- Location of the incident.
- Type of incident (bomb, assassination, et cetera).
- Group claiming responsibility.

Other fields that you may decide to include are:

- Category of the target.
- Nationality of the target.
- Number of victims that were injured.
- Number of victims that were killed.
- Dollar amount of damage reported.
- Number of terrorists killed.
- Number of terrorists injured or captured.

Be sure to include a comment field with enough space for appropriate remarks about each of the records or incidents.

Now you must decide where the information for your incident data base will come from. Start with a major daily newspaper, preferably one with a national and international summary section that lists most bombings and other terrorist actions. If you want to insure that you capture the majority of the incidents that fit the criteria you have defined, it may be to your advantage to subscribe to a clipping service, wire service, or one of the private sector intelligence publications listed in Appendix B.

You should be concerned about the reliability and validity of the information you are collecting. Reliability refers to the need to capture a representative sample of the incidents that fit your criteria. Ideally you would include all of those incidents in your data base, but the cost and commitment required to accomplish that objective may not be cost justified unless you are the U.S. Department of State, the CIA, or the FBI. Besides, a reliable sample of information will provide you with the same basic end products, although the potential margin of error will admittedly be greater than if you captured all of the data.

The degree to which the information you collect is correct is referred to as its validity. Most of the incident information taken from major newspapers or wire services will have a high degree of validity, but before you use information from special-interest publications or groups, or private sector intelligence sources, make sure you know the bias of the organization from whom you are obtaining the information. Some of the so-called intelligence publications on the market are actually used to promote the narrow and extreme interests of the groups that publish them.

If you are concerned with the protection of assets outside of the United States, the U.S. Department of State has an incident data base that can be accessed by private sector organizations that have established their bona fides with that agency. For more information on that service, contact the U.S. Department of State, Overseas Advisory Council (OSAC).

In addition to your incident data base, you will want to maintain hard-copy files on terrorist groups and other subversive organizations that pose a threat to your assets. Private sector firms have more latitude on the information that can be collected and maintained than most public sector agencies and law enforcement departments, especially with respect to information on special-interest groups. In all cases, however, it is important that you make sure you are not violating the legal rights of the individuals or organization on whom you maintain files.

Where does information on these groups and people come from? Again, an important source of information will be the major daily newspapers. You will also want to subscribe to at least one of the major weekly news magazines, such as *Newsweek* or *Time,* and if you have international interests you should also subscribe to the London-based *Economist.* Other sources of information are discussed in Chapter Four and are listed in Appendix B.

Having decided what information you will collect and the sources to be used, the next question to address is who will be responsible for these tasks. In most cases this is not a full-time job, and the responsibility will be assigned to someone working in the security department. Responsibility for the entry of the incident data into the system can be assigned to a clerical employee, but identification of the data (reading the newspapers, magazines, and other information sources), the ordering and reading of special reports on terrorism and terrorist groups, and the development of a weekly or monthly summary should be assigned to a professional security employee who has been given responsibility for becoming a ''terrorism specialist.'' If time constraints and other administrative considerations permit, this specialist should be the person who enters the data into the incident data base, since this activity helps to give that individual a gut-level feeling for the data and its importance to your organization.

TERRORIST TARGET SELECTION

In order to help you think like a terrorist when assessing the threat to your assets, let's again examine how terrorist groups collect information on potential targets, and also reexamine the criteria used by some terrorist leaders when selecting a target.

Unlike our security and law enforcement forces, terrorists are not constrained by ethics or law in the methods they use to collect information and intelligence. They can plant covert listening devices (bugs), torture victims who have information they want, or conduct surveillance on potential targets until they have developed the intelligence needed for their attack. Islamic terrorists in Lebanon subjected CIA station chief William Buckley to extensive torture before he was killed. In the United States a member of the Brotherhood of Silence active support group followed Jewish disk jockey Allen Berg for several days to determine the best time to assassinate him. The assassination was then carried out by other Brotherhood members.

Terrorist groups collect information on potential targets using five basic means of intelligence collection:[1]

- Open-source information.
- Human intelligence collection (HUMINT).
- Signal intelligence collection (SIGINT).
- Surveillance of the target.
- Photographic intelligence collection (PHOTINT).

Open-source information. Jean-Marc Rouillan, leader of the French left-wing Action Direct terrorist group, told a French reporter that most of the information needed to select targets and plan attacks was available in open-source media: the local newspaper, weekly news magazines, and on television and radio. In our open society any alert individual knows what companies are manufacturing weapons or supporting a government in other ways, so that groups such as Action Direct can select and assassinate a figure like a Renault executive because his company is involved in the Strategic Defense Initiative (Star Wars) research. They usually know well in advance when dignitaries are going to visit certain locations. The Provisional Irish Republican Army used this type of information to plan the attempted bombing assassination of British Prime Minister Margaret Thatcher and her cabinet at Brighton in 1984.

Any terrorist group or intelligence cell will find the vast amount of information available in our society to be overwhelming. In the United States, front groups take advantage of the Freedom of Information Act (FOIA) to collect information on the floor plans of government buildings in the U.S. and overseas. They also use FOIA to obtain in-depth information on the various agency functions within our government and the terrorism counteraction plans that law enforcement and other agencies have developed to deal with this problem. They can purchase satellite photographs of many potential targets directly from the United States Geological Survey Division of the Department of the Interior or from either of the two private companies that sell this service. The same sources listed in Appendix B that you can use to get information on terrorism can be used by the terrorists to gather intelligence on U.S. government targets. Companies provide annual reports that include information on their activities and their key executives, some police departments have annuals that include photographs of all the officers in the department, and some military installations and other potential targets have guided tours for the public. Again, the amount of information available to terrorists and other subversives in an open society is overwhelming. The terrorists' biggest problem is sifting through all of this information, deciding what is of use to them and which targets to select.

Human intelligence collection. HUMINT includes intentionally compromising employees of potential targets who have information the group wants or simply initiating a casual conversation at the bar with a disgruntled employee. The other extreme of HUMINT is to kidnap and torture victims who have desired information.

A lot of HUMINT is provided by active and passive supporters of the group's cause. These may include government employees, or employees of private firms with sensitive government contracts, who have access to highly classified information, or simply a worker who may not have access to sensitive information but can provide directions on how to gain access to a particular building or facility.

If the information is considered important enough, a member of a terrorist group intelligence cell may infiltrate an organization by applying for a job with that company or by going to work for a vendor who provides goods or services. Cleaning crews, for example, can gather a tremendous amount of information by collecting trash from the right offices because they have access to the facilities at a time when most other workers are gone.

Signal intelligence collection (SIGINT). A trip to the local Radio Shack will furnish you with all of the components needed to make some very simple transmitters for "bugging" or to use for telephone taps. And while these bugs and taps will cost only a few dollars, the equipment needed to find and neutralize them costs thousands of dollars. If you want more sophisticated electronic surveillance equipment, just visit one of the Miami-based Spy Shops or order what you need from the Executive Protection Products catalog. Whether the device used against you is simple or sophisticated, even when it is found it is almost impossible to know who planted it or how much information was revealed before the bug or tap was detected.

Although only a few terrorist groups may actively engage in the use of bugs or taps, many of them use scanners to monitor police and other public safety radio transmissions.[2] Directories with the frequencies used by most law enforcement departments and government agencies are available in many electronics stores and through the mail. When members of the Brotherhood of Silence were apprehended, for example, almost every member had several scanners that were tuned to monitor the police radios in the areas where they were operating. This allows the terrorists to know when the police are in pursuit of them and also to learn when officers may be called to an area away from the location where a planned attack is about to occur.

Surveillance of the target. Perhaps the second most valuable source of information to the terrorist is collected through simple surveillance. Terrorists sit outside of embassies and note the license plates of both diplomats and employees, and they follow designated targets home after work to locate their residences. They join groups taking public tours of military installations, power plants, government buildings, and other potential targets.

Most terrorist target surveillance is basic. They simply set up their watch in a vehicle or room near the target and observe. But occasionally they become more brazen. Female members of the United Freedom Front went to police stations in the northeastern United States to report a fictitious stolen purse. They were escorted through the entrance of the station and into an interview room, usually on another floor. At some point they asked to use the rest room, and while returning to the interview room they conveniently got lost and wandered around the building. As soon as the terrorist left the police station, she sketched the floor plan. These floor plans were then kept on file for future operations, including the possible need to break out group members who might be arrested and held in those police stations at a later date.

Many terrorist groups watch a number of potential targets and then, when the timing is right, select the best target according to the information collected during the surveillance. In smaller groups, such as the United Freedom Front, the surveillance and the attacks are carried out by the same people. In larger groups, however, an intelligence cell may collect information on a target using surveillance. This information is then used by the leaders, who are located at a safe location, to select a target and plan the attack. Then a tactical cell is committed to the action. An example of this type of operation is the hijacking of the *Achille Lauro*. The ship had been reconnoitered twice by a member of the Palestinian Liberation Front before the decision to proceed with the operation was made by Abu el-Abbas and other leaders of the group. A tactical cell was then infiltrated from Tunisia into Italy and was booked passage on the ship. The rest is history.[3]

Photographic intelligence collection. PHOTINT is used extensively by terrorist intelligence cells for two reasons. First, even if the terrorists collecting the information are the same people who commit to the action, as in the United Freedom Front, they watch a number of targets before they select the one they will attack. When it comes time to make this decision, they use the photographs to refresh their memories as to the unique characteristics of each target.

The second reason that photographic intelligence is so important is that in the larger groups the mission may actually be completed by three independent cells. In the case of the *Achille Lauro,* a one-person cell completed the intelligence mission while taking a cruise on the ship. The leadership of the Palestinian Liberation Front then selected the *Achille Lauro* from among several possible targets. The tactical cell was then committed to the target. Photographic intelligence helps the command cell select targets, and it also helps the tactical personnel to prepare for their part in the mission.

Some groups also collect photographs of counterterrorism forces. They clip pictures from newspapers and magazines of the local SWAT team at a hostage situation, or they attend Armed Forces Day celebrations at military installations where they take pictures of the tactical teams demonstrating rappeling or special operations tactics. This information may be used later to retaliate against members of a team that interferes with an operation, or to "neutralize" a tactical team member or the entire team as part of an attack plan.

When we consider each of these five intelligence collection methods, it becomes apparent that one of the most important aspects of a terrorism counteraction program is awareness—awareness by all employees and other personnel who may observe any of these activities or who may be the targets of an attempted compromise. These people should know how to spot a surveillance team, and they should know to whom to report these activities. In one case a gate guard at a major firm in the United States had been told to record in his log any suspicious activity. He performed his duties faithfully. For three days he recorded all of the activities of three suspicious "Middle Eastern–looking men" who were obviously surveilling and taking pictures of the facility where he worked. But no one ever told him to *report* these activities to anyone, and his logbook was not checked on a regular basis. By the time the company and the appropriate law enforcement agencies became aware of the activity, the three suspicious-looking men had flown back to Beirut with a complete file on that company's facility.

It is important to remember that groups collect information on a number of possible targets before selecting the one they will attack. If you make it difficult to collect information on your assets, you will decrease the probability of an attack. This can be accomplished with good physical and operations security and with an effective employee awareness program.

Interviews with the media and interrogations of captured terrorists and their leaders have provided insight into the criteria used by these people to select their targets. Using the intelligence information collected, the group evaluates potential targets using the following six criteria:

- Criticality of the target.
- Accessibility of the target.
- Recuperability of the target.
- Vulnerability of the target.
- Effect on the terrorist group.
- Risk to the terrorists.

Let's examine these criteria again to make sure that we understand the terrorist mind-set when selecting a target.

Criticality of the target. This is an assessment of the impact that an attack on the target would have on the terrorist's adversary and the surrounding community. Since the objective of most attacks is notoriety and publicity, attacks on utility and communication lines are common. Terrorists get people's attention when they turn off the lights or disrupt telephone service. They also know that detonating a device at a target such as the Rhein Mein Air Force Base in West Germany will result in an awareness among all U.S. and NATO personnel and will demonstrate that a group such as the Red Army Faction can strike at almost any target it chooses.

Accessibility of the target. Can the tactical cell get to the target without being detected and subsequently complete their mission?

Recuperability of the target. The terrorists consider how long the target will be disrupted as a result of their action. If they decide to bomb an electric power transmission line, for example, they would like to target the attack at a point along the transmission line that would take the longest time to repair.

Vulnerability of the target. This is an assessment of what it would actually take to disrupt or destroy the target. How much explosive is needed for a bombing, or how easy would it be for the group to achieve its other short-term goals connected to this action? The Abu Nidal Group recognized the openness and vulnerability of the airports in Rome and Vienna when they planned their attacks at those locations in December 1986, and they also knew that they could achieve their short-term objective (publicity) as a result of these attacks.

Effect on the terrorist group. In the Abu Nidal attacks at the airports in Rome and Vienna, the primary objective was publicity; the group was not concerned with adverse reaction that might be generated because of the murder of innocent people, including women and children. This is not always the case. When the Irish Republican Army assassinated Lord Mountbatten in 1979 and killed his young grand-nephew at the same time, many of the Irish people were appalled. It caused a backlash that resulted in some temporary setbacks in the active and passive support structure of the IRA. The same effect occurred when the FALN planted a bomb in the Fraunces Tavern in New York City that killed four people and injured sixty-three others.[4] The Puerto Rican community denounced the bombing and the other activities of the group. In some cases, the group leaders will consider the public reaction to the attack and the short- and long-term effect that it may have among the active and passive supporters and the general public.

Risk to the terrorists. What is the probability that the tactical cell will be able to escape after the action? This is not always an important consideration, since some terrorists are willing, and in a few cases want, to die for their cause. In other situations the group leaders will commit the cell to a "no-return" mission without telling them that they are not expected to survive.

As an example of these criteria, consider the attack by a lone Islamic terrorist against the U.S. Marine Landing Team barracks in Beirut on 23 October 1983. The target contained one-third of the U.S. Marines in Lebanon, making it a highly critical target. Unfortunately the target was also accessible and vulnerable because of the roads leading up to it and because of the rules of engagement that prevented guards from having ammunition in their weapons. The bomb used by the terrorist was one of the largest nonnuclear devices ever detonated, assuring maximum destruction and almost assuring that the target, the Marine Battalion Landing Team, would never recuperate from the attack. The group was not concerned about the effect on the group because no one ever took credit for the action, which, due to the sophistication of the device used, was undoubtedly a state-sponsored incident. Finally, the risk to the terrorist was not a consideration since this was meant to be a suicide attack. The driver of the vehicle carrying the bomb probably expected to reap his rewards in heaven, where, he had been assured by the Ayatollah Ruholla Khomeini, "God saves the most beautiful virgins for men who die in the Jihad."

Consider the criteria for terrorist target selection when you evaluate attacks on targets similar to the assets you are responsible for protecting. Then relate them directly to your facilities and operations. This will help you to identify information that the groups would like to collect on you, to evaluate your potential as a target, and to plan an effective attack. It should also help you to develop countermeasures to manage this threat.

THREAT INDICATORS

As we have already discussed, a threat assessment is a dynamic process because the threat and the countermeasures used to manage the threat are constantly changing. And since we live in a world where changes are occurring at an extremely rapid pace, it is important that we monitor and modify our assessment on a regular basis. To keep up with possible changes in the threat, many security personnel and terrorism counteraction planners keep their threat assessments on computers using a predetermined list of general and specific threat indicators.

These indicators are entered into your computer using a data-based management software system, and are reviewed on a regular basis. As you conduct the threat assessment using the indicators you have selected, you would place an × or other letter or symbol next to those indicators that apply at that particular time. With a little basic programming, you can then print a list of the indicators you have selected for closer examination, and you can compare your present list with previous assessments. To gain a better understanding of this process, we will examine a list of general and specific threat indicators. Keep in mind, however, that the list you use must be localized according to your needs.

A threat indicator is a condition that, when present, increases the possibility of a terrorist incident. Seldom does one single indicator suggest that the threat is imminent, but when a number of indicators are present, our level of concern should increase correspondingly. Some indicators such as weather are dynamic and constantly changing, whereas others such as terrain are relatively stable. The following is a list of general, local, and specific threat indicators, but once again these should be modified for use by your assets.[5]

General Threat Indicators

1. Political—Unpopular, repressive, or corrupt government.
2. Social—Absence of a middle class in the country or systematic discrimination against specific groups.
3. Economic—Extreme poverty and high unemployment.
4. Ideological—Presence of factions that violently oppose the current political philosophies.
5. Geopolitical—Large foreign populations within the country or active border disputes with neighboring countries.
6. Religious—Presence of ecumenical Marxism, religions that condone and even encourage violence, or other forms of religious strife. These include the radical right Christian Identity churches.

7. Foreign influences—Foreign support for dissident groups or forces of occupation.
8. Present conflict—Low-intensity conflict occurring within the country, even if regionally contained.
9. Opposition to mission—International opposition to the mission assigned to your assets. These include the presence of U.S. forces in many countries and industrial involvement with the Strategic Defense Initiative program.

Local Threat Indicators

1. Dissent for social, political, or ethnic reasons, or resulting from a specific charge brought against the local government.
2. Formation of radical groups, branches of national or subversive groups, or secret societies.
3. Antigovernment and anti-United States agitation and the identification of the local government and/or the U.S. as the root of the local problems.
4. Emergence of new "spokesmen" for the people's causes and arrival of out-of-town organizers and spokespeople in the area.
5. Meetings, rallies, or demonstrations where inflammatory speeches are made and violence is encouraged. This indicator becomes even more critical if local security forces attempt to intervene or counteract these activities and violence occurs.
6. Appearance of antiestablishment posters, leaflets, or other underground press materials designed to incite people.
7. Use of known personalities as a draw to rallies, especially if these people were previously identified with radical causes or groups.
8. Organized civil disobedience where the announced causes are overshadowed by political rhetoric.
9. Increase in recruiting activities by known front groups and other radical organizations.
10. Increased levels of activism at colleges and universities.
11. Speeches and other communiques advocating violence as the *only* solution to the problems discussed.
12. Identification of foreign influences or aid of radical groups to local groups or individuals.

13. Threats against public works, utilities, transportation, and prominent public figures.
14. Agitation in refugee, minority, or foreign communities or other forms of polarization within the population.
15. Reports of stolen firearms, ammunition, and explosives. Raids on armories or sporting goods stores.
16. Violence against property, including looting, destruction, and arson (especially during demonstrations, marches, and other mob actions).
17. Political violence against persons, including murders, attempted murders, beatings, and abductions.
18. Increased purchases of high-performance weapons and the appearance of automatic weapons.
19. Discovery of weapons, ammunition, and explosive caches.
20. Indications of terrorist training or surveillance in the local community.
21. Open attacks on police, military, or other security forces.
22. Terrain around your assets that allows for easy surveillance or access to your facilities or adjacent facilities.

Specific Threat Indicators

1. Current weather is conducive to a terrorist attack.
2. Target has symbolic value.
3. Target is tactically attractive (see pages 87–89 for the criteria for terrorist target selection).
4. Asset is a sensitive installation, for example, nuclear.
5. Asset does not have an antiterrorism program.
6. Asset does not have a counterterrorism capability.
7. Security or police forces are understaffed.
8. Facility lacks direct communication links with security, police, or higher headquarters.
9. Location is in area that is densely populated.
10. Location is in area with easy infiltration and escape routes.
11. Attack on the target would assure maximum publicity.
12. Attacks are occurring against similar targets at other locations.
13. Groups that are currently active have the same ideology as groups that are capable of operating in your area.
14. There is currently a high level of terrorist activity at several different locations around the world.

15. Terrorist groups are active in the immediate area.
16. Terrorist groups have attacked this target in the past.

As we previously discussed, when collecting, analyzing, and maintaining the information used to evaluate these indicators, make sure that you do not violate any of the standards, regulations, or laws that govern your operations and the rights of the various groups and individuals. For example, police agencies cannot maintain files on individuals because they belong to organizations that are simply antiestablishment, and military facilities may be limited to maintaining files only on individuals or groups that present an actual and current threat to that facility.

These threat indicators will be revised according to your situation and needs. You should review your list of indicators at least every six months to determine if the threat level is increasing or decreasing. Responsibility for this activity should be assigned to a security, intelligence, or law enforcement professional who will prepare an intelligence summary as part of your threat statement for distribution to the entire threat management committee each time an assessment is completed. It is recommended that the same person conduct all of the threat assessments so that this individual develops some degree of expertise in this area. Other members of the threat management committee should review the list of indicators every six to twelve months and recommend any additions or deletions.

When a threat assessment is conducted using these indicators, the person doing the assessment should prepare a list of only those indicators that are valid at the time the assessment is conducted rather than simply using a standard form for every assessment. Preparing a separate list helps to insure that changes in the threat level and the reasons for these changes are readily identified. This process also makes it easier for you to identify changes that occur between assessments and to know immediately if the threat is increasing, decreasing, or remaining constant. As we discussed, if the indicators are programmed into your computer, this process is greatly simplified.

VULNERABILITY DETERMINATION

A threat assessment considers the entire milieu in which your facilities and other assets exist. One important aspect of that milieu focuses on the vulnerability of those facilities and assets. A vulnerability determination is a systematic approach to evaluating the assailability of a potential target based on the use of an established set of criteria. For our purposes we will use three separate sets, one based on the criteria for terrorist target selection and two based on projects conducted by the U.S. military. These systems are provided as examples. It is up to you to localize them according to your needs.

Let's begin by once again looking at the criteria that terrorist leaders use to select their targets. However, this time we will put the criteria into a question format; the more "yes" answers you check, the greater your vulnerability to being selected as a target.

Criteria	Yes	No
1. Would the destruction or disruption of this facility have a great impact on the immediate community or the national government? (Also, check yes if there is a historic or national landmark.)	___	___
2. Is this facility easily accessible or are adjoining buildings accessible?	___	___
3. If this facility were attacked, would it take a considerable amount of time and effort for the community to recuperate?	___	___
4. Would it be fairly easy to destroy or disrupt this facility (vulnerability)?	___	___
5. Is there little likelihood that an attack on this target would result in a public backlash against the terrorists or their cause?	___	___
6. If a terrorist group were to select this target, is there a good chance that the tactical cell would escape?	___	___

If you checked "yes" to all six questions, and if there is a terrorist threat in your area, then you may be vulnerable to an attack. So what can you do to reduce your vulnerability? Let's use the first question on the list to explore the possibilities.

If the destruction or disruption of this facility would have a major impact on the community or the national government, there is probably nothing you can do to change that fact. As a result you must develop other approaches to managing this aspect of your threat and vulnerability. Begin with an effective operations security program and deny your terrorist adversaries the information they need to make this determination. Obviously it isn't advisable to announce to the world the degree of "criticality" you offer as a target. But since the terrorists may already have this information, the alternative defense action is to keep them from collecting the intelligence needed to plan an attack. Again, good operations security is an important element of managing the threat, along with good physical security, communications and document control, and access control.

Be creative in managing your vulnerability once it is defined. If your facility is easily accessible, develop methods for decreasing that accessibility. At the Marine Landing Team barracks in Beirut, a few barriers in the road, or concrete abutments that would have forced the driver to slow down and maneuver around them, may have made a difference. Instead, an almost straight road with no barriers allowed the suicide terrorist to build up speed and crash into the building itself before detonating his explosives.

The U.S. military has developed several vulnerability-determining systems. You can use the basic criteria from these approaches to develop your own vulnerability-determining system, but make sure that you do not develop a ''points mentality.'' Each of these systems has a point score range from 0 to 100, with 100 indicating the greatest degree of vulnerability. However, a higher score doesn't necessarily mean that you are in immediate danger of attack. There are a number of other important variables to consider. For example, if there are no terrorist groups operating in your area, then the overall threat and vulnerability may be minimal. On the other hand, if you have a low vulnerability score but there is substantial activity in your area, then the interaction between the threat level and your vulnerability may suggest that you need to adopt special measures to harden the assets you are responsible for protecting.

The **Installation Vulnerability-Determining System** (IVDS)[6] was originally designed in the 1970s to assess the vulnerability of a fixed installation in the United States. A modified version of the complete system, including instructions, is found in Appendix C. The major criteria evaluated by the system include:

- Installation characteristics and sensitivity.
- Status of terrorism counteraction training.
- Availability of communications.
- Availability of outside security or law enforcement assistance.
- Time and distance from other military installations.
- Time and distance from urban areas.
- Geographic region (location).
- Proximity to foreign borders.

• Access to the installation.
• Population density of the installation.
• Terrain.

The **Unit Vulnerability Assessment** (UVA)[7] was developed as part of a joint U.S. Marine–U.S. Army project following the Beirut incident. It focuses on the vulnerability of small units being deployed into countries around the world where different levels of conflict may be present. A modified version of the UVA, which is found in Appendix D, includes three major areas of assessment and fifteen subsections.

General Assessment

• Unit mission sensitivity.
• VIPs.
• Current threat analysis.
• World attitude to mission.
• Status of unit training.
• Unity of security effort.

Regional Assessment

• Area of deployment.
• Availability of intelligence and security advice.
• Other U.S. military assistance.

Specific Location Assessment

• Availability of outside law enforcement or security assistance.
• Location.
• Access to the location.
• Personnel/vehicle access.
• Communications.
• Tactical limitations (restricted rules of engagement).

OTHER THREAT ASSESSMENT TECHNIQUES

Another important technique used for threat assessments is the **development of scenarios** that are specific to your assets. The best scenarios are based on actual incidents that have occurred, hopefully, at other locations. Monitor the tactics and techniques used by groups elsewhere and ask how those same approaches might be used to target your facility; then develop scenarios based on these analyses.

You may also use your creativity and think like a terrorist as you develop scenarios based on your own vulnerabilities, even if the tactics and strategies in the scenario have not yet been used during previous attacks. Your adversary is highly creative and constantly looking for and planning new methods. By using this approach you may stay one step ahead of him in preventing an attack from occurring or at least decreasing the probability of the success of that attack.

Once you have developed your scenarios, review them with the entire threat management committee. Compare the scenarios with the current threat and vulnerability assessments to determine how realistic they are and, more importantly, to develop plans for preventing them from occurring. You may also use these scenarios for another important threat assessment technique, "war gaming."

As we discussed in the previous chapter, **war gaming** includes both desktop and field exercises, and it is an excellent approach to validating your terrorism counteraction plans. For a command post exercise (CPX) or desktop exercise, have your emergency operations center work through the scenario as though it were actually occurring. You will want to appoint several people to plan, monitor, and evaluate the exercise and the performance of the emergency operations or crisis management team. The problem with most exercises is that not enough time is allocated for them. An exercise that ends in an hour or two doesn't allow you to evaluate the effects of stress and fatigue and their impact on the team's functioning, nor does it allow for the dominant personality to emerge or personality conflicts to occur, as they sometimes do in a long-term, high-stress situation. Ideally, the exercise would last for several days. However, if you can allow a full day to the CPX, then you are doing better than many organizations.

Your war game and terrorism counteraction plan validation can be fully tested if you will commit to a **complete field training exercise** (FTX). During an FTX you include all of the security and law enforcement assets that would be committed during an actual incident, including tactical teams, hostage negotiators, patrol officers, and the command team. You will want a tactical team or other personnel from outside the facility to act as the adversaries or would-be terrorists. The adversaries may plant dummy bombs and take hostages during the FTX. Again, a major con-

98 THE ANTITERRORISM HANDBOOK

sideration will be the time required to complete the exercise, especially considering the number of people committed to an FTX, but if you can allow a full twelve to fifteen hours for the exercise you will achieve most of your objectives: All of the personnel involved in your counterterrorism response planning will be able to participate and many of the personal and interpersonal dynamics that often take place during an actual event will be experienced.

You may want to use another agency or **outside consultants** to assist you in conducting your threat assessment activities. These professionals may be able to develop your specific threat assessment materials, conduct your initial assessment, and then train your personnel to complete these tasks. Consultants can also be used to provide awareness training for all of your personnel if you do not have this expertise in-house.

If you have a sensitive installation, you may also want to consider the use of **penetration teams** to test your security. These teams will attempt to compromise and breach your security. Penetration teams are normally used only in special situations since the team must be highly trained and know how to respond if they are detected. More importantly, they must have the proper security clearance to access the facilities that they attempt to penetrate. In most cases these teams are not used against private sector facilities unless those facilities are involved in nuclear or military contracts.

MAKING IT WORK

To complete your threat assessment you need to:

1. Identify and learn as much as you can about the terrorist groups that pose a threat to your assets.
2. Develop and use a list of threat indicators.
3. Develop and use a vulnerability-determining system.
4. Develop scenarios that are specific to the assets you are protecting.
5. Validate your assessments and operational plans through the use of war gaming and the other techniques discussed.

For your threat assessment to remain dynamic and to insure the effectiveness of all your terrorism counteraction plans, you must have an appropriate state of awareness at all levels within the organization. Employees and other personnel must know that terrorists collect information on potential targets, they need to understand how this information is collected, and they need to know whom to report suspicious activities to if they see or hear anything out of the ordinary.

Finally, you may want to relate your threat assessment and the current level of threat to a response system. For example, during the initial development of terrorism counteraction planning within the U.S. military, three levels of threat condition were formulated: Threat Condition White, Threat Condition Yellow, and Threat Condition Red. Although the military has since expanded these alert conditions to include THREATCON ALPHA through THREATCON DELTA, the original concept is easily modified for use by government agencies and corporations.[8]

Threat Condition White. Nonspecific threat of terrorism against your assets.

Recommended Actions

1. Encourage community security awareness of suspicious persons, vehicles, and activities.
2. Review terrorism counteraction security plans and verify the availability of your reaction forces.
3. Spot-check vehicles and randomly check the identification of persons entering the installation or area.
4. Exercise bomb threat procedures.
5. Monitor all deliveries to the facility.
6. Periodically check buildings and facilities not in regular use.
7. Implement appropriate security measures for high-risk personnel.

Threat Condition Yellow. Specific threat of terrorism against your assets.

Recommended Actions

1. Review antiterrorism plans and implement appropriate measures.
2. Brief all personnel on the threat condition and emphasize security awareness.
3. Tighten control of entry to installations.
   a. Conduct a random check of vehicles, packages, suitcases, and handbags carried into the installation.
   b. Conduct a random check of personnel identification.

     c. For controlled-access facilities, implement a 100 percent iden-
       tification check.
4. Increase checks during off-duty hours of buildings, installations,
   and perimeters.
5. Implement appropriate security measures for high-risk personnel.
6. Review and brief all security personnel to directives and regulations concerning the use of deadly force.

Threat Condition Red. Imminent threat of terrorist acts against your assets.

Recommended Actions

1. Appropriate actions under Threat Conditions White and Yellow
   that are not already in effect.
2. Place on call and brief reaction forces.
3. Inspect and search all vehicles and containers entering the facility.
4. Increase security of threatened and/or sensitive facilities.
     a. Inspect all packages, suitcases, and handbags entering the area.
     b. Strictly enforce parking regulations and, if possible, prevent
       parking immediately adjacent to high-threat buildings or areas.
     c. Increase the frequency of perimeter patrols and other security
       activities.
5. Man all required security posts.
6. As required, provide personnel protection for high-risk personnel.

The threat assessment provides the foundation for the rest of your terrorism counteraction program. Next, we will discuss some of the antiterrorism approaches used to "harden" your assets and also what you should expect in the event that you need to activate your counterterrorism response plans. Keep in mind as we discuss operations security, personnel security, and physical security that this handbook is not meant to provide a complete overview on any of these areas. It should help you understand how to approach each security need from an antiterrorism perspective, building on basic security measures that should already be in place.

IMPLEMENTATION CHECKLIST

1. Establish your terrorism incident data base.
   a. Determine the sources of your data.
   b. Evaluate the reliability and validity of the information available from those sources.
   c. Assign responsibility for this activity to a "terrorism specialist."
2. Consider measures to counter terrorist intelligence collection methods.
   a. Open-source information.
   b. Human intelligence collection.
   c. Signal intelligence collection.
   d. Surveillance of the target.
   e. Photographic intelligence collection.
3. Review the criteria for terrorist target selection. How many of these apply to your assets and what can you do to counter these threats?
4. Develop a localized threat indicator checklist and assign responsibility for conducting a threat assessment using this checklist to a member of the threat management committee.
5. Develop your vulnerability-determination checklist using the following information as models:
   a. Terrorist target selection criteria.
   b. Installation Vulnerability-Determining System.
   c. Unit Vulnerability Assessment.
6. Review the scenarios you have developed.
   a. Develop additional scenarios using your creativity rather than previous incidents as the basis. If you were a terrorist, how would you attack your installation?
   b. Compare your scenarios to your threat indicators and vulnerability-determining systems.
7. Validate your scenarios and countermeasures using:
   a. Desktop exercises.
   b. Field training exercises.
   c. Review by consultants.
   d. Use of penetration teams.
8. Prepare a threat condition level format with required responses at each level.

CHAPTER SIX

Operations Security

SCENARIO

Except for the military representative, the members of the threat management committee had never heard of operations security. Lieutenant Colonel Marsh explained to them that, just as their committee was collecting information on the APP and the Citizens Against Chemical Warfare, it was a good bet that at least one if not both of these groups was also collecting information on them and the organizations they represented. Operations security, or OPSEC, was the process of denying the groups the information they were seeking.

Lieutenant Colonel Marsh explained the process: "First, we have to identify the information, or elements of information, that the groups would like to collect on us. These are referred to as the essential elements of friendly information, or EEFI. Next, we decide what intelligence or information collection techniques could be used to obtain that information. Then we identify the countermeasures we can use to prevent that information from being compromised. OPSEC is simply denying your adversaries the information they need to plan an attack against you, and doing everything possible to make your activities appear to be unpredictable."

The committee decided to spend the rest of this week's meeting using brainstorming techniques to develop their list of EEFI. The list compiled during the session was overwhelming. It included bits and pieces of information about the committee and each organization represented that could be of use to a hostile intelligence service or a terrorist intelligence cell. Rosters of employees, contractors, and vendors; security procedures; housing accommodations; information on the research being conducted at the base; and the activities of the committee itself were all on the list of EEFI.

The committee stayed through most of the day, long after the meeting was scheduled to end, and also brainstormed a list of methods and procedures that an intelligence agent or cell could use to attempt to obtain the information listed on the EEFI. Again the list was extensive. There were numerous ways that a trained terrorist cell or other adversary could collect all of the information needed to identify major vulnerabilities and plan a successful attack.

After the meeting finally broke up, Charlie Fox sat in the conference room reviewing the day's activities and looking at the lists of EEFI and the methods that could be used to compromise them. The lists had been posted on chart paper and taped to the walls around him. In his solitude the potential gravity of the threat to his community began to sink in once again. For years the department had done an excellent job performing its normal police functions, but security at the department and at other community locations had been lax, and operations security in particular was almost nonexistent. Information on the personnel working for each of the organizations represented on the committee was readily available to anyone who asked for it. Floor plans of all the buildings and aerial photographs of the entire city were available from government agencies, and background checks of many of the key employees had never been properly conducted. Charlie felt like the Dutch boy with his finger in the dike, trying to hold back the onslaught of the entire North Sea.

At next week's brainstorming session the threat management committee would list countermeasures that could be implemented to improve its operations security program. John Filmore had experience in electronic surveillance and countermeasures, so he was asked to consider threats and OPSEC procedures in that area. Lieutenant Colonel Marsh would assess the need for OPSEC surveys to identify predictable behaviors and procedures, and measures to counter those threats. Other committee members had also been assigned specific areas to research and present to the committee during next week's session. Then the committee could begin to put these measures into practice. Charlie hoped they had enough time.

Jack Pardue was listening to the tapes of that day's threat management committee meeting. He had the tapes in hand, along with photographs of the committee members, within four hours of the end of the meeting. OPSEC was not new to Jack. He had learned about it while in the Army and had long ago implemented OPSEC procedures within the APP. He was surprised that ZOG had taken so long to recognize the value of OPSEC, but frankly it was too late. Jack already had the information needed to plan his attacks in Pleasantville. His plan was guaranteed to get ZOG's attention and earn the APP the recognition it deserved.

He wasn't going to strike at secure areas anyway; the school was his primary target. An APP tactical cell carrying explosives and automatic weapons could easily breach the perimeter fence near the school and take several classrooms of students as hostages. The tactical cell would be told that the hostages would be used to attract media attention for their cause and to bargain for a helicopter to be used for the cell's escape. They were not to use their weapons or detonate their explosives unless they had to.

In reality Jack's plan was to play the incident as long as he could and then radio detonate the explosives carried by the tactical team. The APP would gain martyrs and victims at the same time. It would show the world that they were as committed to their cause as the Abu Nidal members who massacred civilians at the Rome and Vienna airports or the PLO terrorists who seized a high school and assassinated twenty-one children in 1974 at Maalot, Israel. All of the Aryan children would be released at the beginning of the hostage-taking so that none of the future warriors of Jack's revolution would be lost. The action would take place in four weeks—the Friday before Armed Forces Day.

James Raskin, executive secretary of the Citizens Against Chemical Warfare, was also thinking about Pleasantville. He had decided to form a chapter there, and his Cuban DGI contact had agreed that the Friday before Armed Forces Day would be the ideal time for their initial demonstration in the community, since the authorities there would expect them to show up on Armed Forces Day. By arriving a day early, they would catch them off guard. The demonstrators would meet in a town a hundred miles from Pleasantville and then be bused to the demonstration. They anticipated 100-plus demonstrators, including several "professionals" who would in-sure that the atmosphere would turn violent.

If all went as planned, the buses would arrive at the front gate of Fort Richardson at 7 A.M. on Friday morning, just as the guard was changing shifts. The media would be immediately notified of the group's arrival, and the initial activities would be limited to picketing and chanting in the parking lot across from the front gate. Eventually the demonstrators would block traffic by staging a sit-in at the front gate, and when security officers or police attempted to move them, demonstrators who remained in the parking lot area would begin throwing eggs at the authorities.

The ultimate plan was for the demonstration to become violent. The professional demonstrators would remain at the rear of the parking lot crowd and, when the time was right, they would use slingshots to propel cherry bombs dipped in glue and BBs over the demonstrators. The cherry bombs would be lit with their cigarettes as they were about to shoot them, and would explode over the heads of the police and security officers and the front lines of the demonstrators. Then canisters of tear gas would be rolled into the crowd and strings of firecrackers would be set off.

Raskin was counting on the local television stations to cover the events with their "live eye" camera. That way he could observe the demonstration, as it occurred, from his hotel room 100 miles away.

*   *   *

Terrorists don't just get up in the morning and decide to hijack an ocean liner, place a bomb on an airplane, or assassinate a public official. A tremendous amount of intelligence collection, planning, and preparation goes into almost every action. In order to operate with some potential degree of success, they must have as much information as they can obtain about their targets so that they are able to identify and take advantage of the targets' vulnerable areas. They must also have some knowledge of the targets' ability to respond to their attack, including damage control and tactical response capabilities.

Terrorist groups are most vulnerable during three of their five operational phases. During the preincident phase they must be able to collect intelligence on the target. This intelligence includes information on your security practices, vulnerabilities, and your potential to respond to an incident if you are targeted. By developing a good operations security program, you can deny the terrorists this information. And if you combine the operations security program with an effective counterintelligence capability, you may be lucky enough to identify and apprehend the terrorist intelligence cell during this phase.

Terrorists are also vulnerable as they move to the target during the initiation phase. If the intelligence they initially collected was incorrect or incomplete, they may be detected and apprehended during this phase. The "denial, disguise, and deception" components of an effective operations security program can, if properly conducted, increase their vulnerability at this point.[1]

During the escape phase of the operation the terrorists must have the ability to predict your response capabilities and they must have knowledge of the security and law enforcement units and personnel they may confront. Again, a properly executed operations security program can prevent them from gaining this information.

Operations security (OPSEC) is defined by U.S. Army Regulation 530-1 (15 October 1985) as "the process of denying adversaries information about friendly capabilities and intentions by identifying, controlling, and predicting indicators associated with the planning and conducting of military operations and other activities." [2] When attempting to manage the threat of terrorism, operations security is an important consideration for law enforcement and for other private and public sector organizations as well as for the military.

The basic objective of an operations security program is to deny terrorists the opportunity to collect information on your activity and to prevent them from developing intelligence that would allow them to predict your actions. The ultimate objective of the OPSEC program is to significantly increase the risk to the terrorists so that they will select an alternative target.[3] We must remember, however, that some of today's groups include members who are willing to commit to a suicide mission, and that some leaders are willing to commit a tactical cell to a suicide mission even when the members of the cell are not aware of the commitment. So, although the best operations security program in the world may significantly increase the risk to the terrorists, they may still target your facility if they feel the objectives of the operation outweigh the risks involved.

Consider, for example, the car bomb attacks on Israeli checkpoints in southern Lebanon during their occupation of the region. The Israeli security at these checkpoints was at a high state of alert at all times, but by the very nature of their activity the soldiers manning those positions had to accept a certain amount of risk when they stopped and checked vehicles. On several occasions, highly committed (or coerced) Shiites drove up to a checkpoint in a vehicle full of explosives, which, when detonated, killed the terrorist and the soldiers. Even when the times and locations of the vehicle checks were randomized (a standard OPSEC procedure), a committed bomber could just keep driving around until he was eventually stopped by Israeli soldiers.

In order to develop an effective operations security program, you must have as much knowledge as you can obtain about the intelligence collection and operational capabilities of the terrorists who might target your activity. Then, as you develop your program, think like a terrorist member of those groups. In other words, look at your operations from the perspective of a terrorist who is collecting intelligence and planning an operation against you.

OPERATIONS SECURITY INDICATORS

The first step in developing your operations security program is to identify the information that must be protected. The second step is to identify the techniques your adversary might use to compromise that information. The final step is to develop the approaches you can use to prevent the second step from occurring. Have your threat management committee, or other appropriate group, brainstorm each of these steps. Remember when brainstorming that initially there are no bad ideas. Every idea or suggestion generated should be written down on chart paper; after you have completed your brainstorming you can go back and evaluate each idea listed. It is best to allow at least a day for each step of your OPSEC program development and allow a week between each brainstorming session.

During the first week's session, develop a list of operations security indicators. During the second week's session, concentrate on developing a list of methods that terrorists would use to compromise each indicator. During the final brainstorming session in the third week, develop a list of potential countermeasures. By allowing a week between each session, you permit committee members to think of other items that were not identified during the previous session. Obviously, if you are developing an operations security program for a large installation or a series of activities, it might take you more than one day to complete each step.

The indicators you list during the initial session are referred to as "essential elements of friendly information." As we have discussed, many of these elements are available through open sources. Information on the company president is found in almost every annual report. City halls publish the weekly itinerary for the mayor, and most installation newspapers include stories about the commanding officer and visiting dignitaries. To insure that you have a dynamic and ongoing collection of EEFI, your committee should collect and review all open-source information on the assets you are responsible for protecting and review this information from the adversary's perspective.

Examples of operations security indicators or EEFI include:

- Names of your employees.
- Identification and routine of vendors.
- Physical layout of your facility.
- Security measures and routines.
- Names of key executives and dignitaries.
- Operational patterns within the facility.
- Stereotyped procedures.
- Who parks in which parking space.
- Travel plans for key people.
- Locations of private residences.
- Information on family members.
- Methods of communications.
- Liaisons with outside law enforcement/security forces.
- Contingency plans, including crisis management planning.
- Access control methods you are using.
- Methods used to secure sensitive/classified information.
- Utility control points.
- Future plans and activities.

DEFINING THE THREAT

Intelligence used by terrorist groups may be collected by an intelligence cell of active cadre, by active or passive supporters, or even by professional agents employed by the group's sponsoring state. Although much of the information is collected through **open sources,** terrorists also use a number of other methods to obtain information that is not as readily available. Let's discuss these methods again, this time from the perspective of an effective OPSEC program.

Human intelligence collection (HUMINT) is the second most frequently used method (open-source information is first). Some HUMINT is also collected through overt, or open, sources. Active and passive supporters may have access through their jobs or other connections to information that the group needs. Disgruntled employees or individuals who recently left an organization may be willing to provide information. And in some cases, information may be purchased from people who have access to it.

HUMINT can also be collected using covert sources. The group, for example, may assign a member of an intelligence cell the mission of infiltrating an organization. The member will obtain a job with the target and then obtain the information the group is seeking.

Another approach to HUMINT involves clandestine collection operations. These operations are expensive and time consuming and are designed to develop agents among the existing employees or other people who have access to the information needed on the target organization. Because of the time involved and the potential for discovery, clandestine operations are not usually used by terrorist groups unless the information needed justifies the risks involved. Besides, it may be more convenient for the group to identify an individual with the information they need, kidnap that person, and extract the information using any means at their disposal, including torture. This approach was used by the group in Lebanon that kidnapped, tortured, and murdered William Buckley, the CIA station chief in Beirut.

Another major source of intelligence collection is **imagery collection,** including **photographic intelligence collection (PHOTINT).** Remember that the leadership who decides which targets to attack often remains in a safe haven and does not conduct the actual reconnaissance; a good set of photographs helps them to evaluate the potential targets during their selection and planning process. The group may also have access to satellite photos, either from a sponsoring state or from one of the commercial firms that provides this service. Your OPSEC program should include procedures for limiting the potential for photographing your sensitive areas and procedures.

Many groups also have the capability of compromising your communications and gaining information. They can tap your telephones, plant listening devices (bugs) in strategic locations, and even use highly technical approaches to conduct **signal intelligence collection (SIGINT).** While the telephone is usually your most vulnerable point with respect to SIGINT, there are a number of other methods available to state-sponsored terrorists, including the potential capability to monitor information that is entered into your computers.

Not all terrorist groups have access to the sophisticated equipment needed to perform exotic SIGINT collection. But in most cases this equipment is not needed. The information required to evaluate a target and plan an attack can be collected by (1) gathering all of the open-source information available on the target, (2) observing the target for several days, and (3) photographing all of the key elements, procedures, and personnel at the target.

COUNTERMEASURES

After identifying the essential elements of friendly information (EEFI) and reviewing the methods used by terrorists to collect this information, the next step is to evaluate, select, and implement the countermeasures needed to manage the OPSEC threat. It is best to begin this process by first evaluating the security programs and procedures you currently have in operation. Where possible, integrate OPSEC into these procedures and then develop specific OPSEC approaches to address those areas that remain vulnerable.

One of the programs that should be evaluated involves your information security procedures. What information is released to the public, what information is readily available, and what information is protected? Remember that a key part of your OPSEC program is to have one committee member monitor all open-source information on the assets you are protecting and evaluate that information from the perspective of a terrorist intelligence collection cell.

Another consideration is to review the communications security methods you are using. Is sensitive information discussed on the telephone at the office or from an executive's home? In either case, this information could be easily compromised. This is a special threat because it is so easy to tap into telephone conversations, yet it is impossible to conduct business on a day-to-day basis without discussing important information on the telephone.

As our society continues to become more technological and information oriented, computers and information management systems are becoming attractive targets to terrorists and increasingly vulnerable to attack. The damage that a single hacker can cause was demonstrated in 1988 when a Cornell University graduate student, Robert Tappan Morris, introduced a "virus" into a network that included university and military computers. His virus affected more than 6,000 computers and caused portions of the network to shut down for several days.

Physical security, and access control in particular, is an important OPSEC consideration. Try to make it difficult for the collection cell to predict whom you will check as they enter a selected area. If you are securing a major installation, for example, stop all blue cars on Tuesday and on Thursday stop all cars with license plates beginning with the letter E. The following week, use different criteria. Try to be as unpredictable as possible by using random criteria to decide upon your daily security activities. If you are securing a building, stop everyone with blue trousers or a blue skirt on Monday and everyone with brown shoes on Wednesday. Then select new and unpredictable criteria for next week. Of course the ultimate access control approach is to check everyone and every vehicle at all times, but this is not always practical or possible.

Make sure you introduce OPSEC into your personnel security programs. People should know that surveillance and photography are key elements in most intelligence collection programs. They should be watching for these activities, and if they observe any unusual people or situations they must know to whom to report them. They should also report any attempts by friends or neighbors to find out even the most basic information about your operations and vulnerabilities. Even the neighbor they have known for years could have suddenly identified with the group's cause and now be part of the active or passive support group.

Once you have integrated OPSEC considerations into your other security programs, you should review your list of EEFI and approaches to compromising those elements and develop some specific OPSEC procedures to address those areas where you are still vulnerable. Where appropriate, consider the three "Ds" of OPSEC: **denial, disguise,** and **deception.** As much as possible, deny your adversary the opportunity to collect information on your operations and procedures. Since it is impossible to deny access to all information, you may disguise procedures or methods so that they are more difficult to detect. The use of plain-clothes security personnel in addition to uniformed people makes it more difficult to assess your total security posture. The gate or fence that appears to be vulnerable may actually be reinforced with cable or other materials that make it difficult to penetrate, even when approached by a speeding truck. And finally, consider the use of deception. For example, when moving sensitive materials such as nuclear or chemical agents, some of the trucks and railway cars could actually be empty. Even the drivers and the guards would not know which containers held the sensitive materials. This deception would significantly decrease the possibility of a terrorist group orchestrating a successful attack to steal these materials.

IMPLEMENTATION CHECKLIST

1. Conduct a brainstorming session to identify your "essential elements of friendly information" (EEFI).
   a. Identify all possible bits and pieces of information of value to your adversary.
   b. Schedule brainstorming sessions with at least a one-week interval between each session.
2. Conduct a brainstorming session to identify methods that could be used to compromise your EEFI.
   a. Think like a terrorist as you go through this process.
   b. Emphasize the information available through open sources of information.
3. Conduct a brainstorming session to identify methods that can be used to counter your OPSEC threat. Be sure to consider:
   a. Information security procedures.
   b. Communication security.
   c. Physical security.
   d. The three "Ds."

CHAPTER SEVEN

Personnel Security

SCENARIO

The members of the threat management committee were worried. Intelligence on the Aryan Peoples Party and the Citizens Against Chemical Warfare had dried up. There had been no new concrete information for the past week and Armed Forces Day was just two weeks away. The last information they had received indicated that both groups might be planning some type of activity for that day. Dave Nelson assured everyone that the FBI would stay on top of the situation and that if any evidence emerged that a demonstration, bombing, or attack was imminent, he would notify everyone immediately.

Charlie Fox spoke up in support of Dave Nelson. "Dave and the bureau have done a good job so far of keeping us informed. I think we should leave the intelligence collection to the FBI and continue to concentrate on developing our antiterrorism programs. We have a lot to accomplish, and it's just two weeks to Armed Forces Day. Right now my biggest concern is our lack of personnel security. We haven't even identified the potential targets that these groups might go after."

"Good point." Nelson was happy to move on to another topic. "The Citizens Against Chemical Warfare doesn't target individuals, but we know that the APP has a hit list, and several key people from Pleasantville are on it."

John Filmore from Toten Industries asked Nelson for more specific information. Was the president of his company on the list, or had he himself achieved the dubious honor?

"The last information we received indicated that Mayor Wilson, the commander of Fort Richardson, and possibly Chief Casey were on the list. No one from Toten was included."

"How about Sheriff Potter?" Filmore responded. "You know, the APP compound is actually located in his jurisdiction, and I'm concerned about the fact that we haven't included him on this committee."

Charlie Fox explained that there was a need to keep this committee's activities as low key and quiet as possible. "Dave and I were afraid that if the sheriff's department was included on the committee, word on all our actions would leak directly to Jack Pardue. We have reason to believe that the department has APP supporters at the highest level." In spite of pleading from the other committee members, Fox and Nelson would not discuss the reasons for their concerns.

"Let's get to work," said Charlie. He wanted to get the discussion back on track. "We need to make a list of people who may be targeted and then divide that list into three categories—people who would be specifically targeted, people who are part of a group that might be targeted, and random targets."

Within an hour the group had an "A" list that included the mayor, the police chief, the Fort Richardson commander, and the president of Toten Industries. The "B" list included police and security officers, military personnel, scientists working at Fort Richardson, Toten managers, and the members of their committee. The group decided not to develop a "C" list, since little could be done to directly counter the threat to that group and they felt it best to concentrate their resources on the A and B lists.

Members of the committee were assigned responsibility for preparing crisis management and location files for each person on the A list. These files would include personal information on those people and their families, and floor plans of the residences and offices.

Lieutenant Colonel Bob Marsh volunteered to develop and present a special three-hour training session on personal protection. The training would show people on the A and B lists how to recognize surveillance, what to do if they thought they were in danger of attack, and how to decrease the probability of being targeted by an extremist group. The Army had provided Marsh with a set of slides he used for his military briefings, but he felt that they might be too graphic for a civilian presentation. The committee members agreed that pictures of body parts weren't needed to get the point across. They decided to keep the training low key.

The final task at this week's meeting was to identify police officers and security personnel who had been trained to work on personal protection details. Fort Richardson had four military police who had been trained by the Army Criminal Investigation Division (CID). Toten had two ex-military security guards who had been trained some time ago, and the police department had four people who had attended a Secret Service training program. It was obvious that if the threat level increased and all of the people on the A list needed protection, the TMC did not have the resources to provide it. Sara Lyndon agreed to contact the local Secret Service office and arrange for a training session. Sara was the best liaison for this job since the BATF and Secret Service were both under the Department of the Treasury and worked closely together.

Jack Pardue's plans were finalized. He also had an A list, and the name at the top was Sheriff Potter. The sheriff's assassination would demonstrate that even ZOG's protectors weren't safe from his wrath, and it would provide for a diversion while they hit their primary target—the Fort Richardson school.

The attack on the school was scheduled for 8:30 A.M. on the Friday before Armed Forces Day. Pardue also wanted to attack city hall and the federal building at the same time, but he didn't have enough tactical personnel to commit to more than one attack. Jack decided that casualties and martyrs at the school would result in the most publicity for his cause.

But the other targets weren't forgotten. The APP would plant bombs at Toten Industries and city hall. They would also place explosive devices in police and FBI automobiles. All of these would explode as APP members were taking their hostages at the school. This would be a Friday that history would long remember. Armageddon is now!

James Raskin set the phone receiver back into its cradle, having just finished talking to his contact in Pleasantville. He now had a chapter of Citizens Against Chemical Warfare there, and the demonstration was set for the Friday before Armed Forces Day. Raskin had also enlisted the support of two well-known media personnel and a clergyman, who agreed to attend the demonstration. All three of these people had been associated with socialist causes for years and their presence, along with the special activities Raskin had planned, would guarantee the publicity he was seeking. Raskin began making the final preparations for the Pleasantville demonstration.

*   *   *

In recent years there has been an alarming trend: Each terrorist attack is planned specifically to injure, maim, and kill as many people as possible.

Also, the trend has been to kill more kidnap and hostage victims. A terrorism counteraction program must include procedures for preventing attacks against your personnel and for doing everything possible to insure their survival if they are involved in a terrorist action.

Personnel targeted by terrorists fall into three basic categories.

1. **Selection of a specific person.** In this case the adversary has selected a specific victim, usually because of that person's rank or position. The individual may be selected for assassination or for a kidnapping incident. Examples include the selection of Hans Beckhurts for assassination by the Red Army Faction because his company was involved in certain defense contracts, or Brig. Gen. James Dozier for kidnapping by the Brigate Rosse because of his position within NATO.

2. **Selection of a specific group of people.** Here the terrorist objective is to target a group of people falling into a specific category without reference to any one individual within the group. Persons might be selected because they are U.S. military personnel, Israeli citizens, or members of a minority group. The La Belle discotheque in Berlin was bombed in 1986 because it was a hangout for U.S. citizens—the group targeted by the state that sponsored the bombing (Libya). And when Arab terrorists hijacked an Egyptian airliner to Malta, they intentionally selected Israeli and American women for assassination.

3. **Random victims.** In this case the terrorists don't care who the victims are, they just want people to die. The series of bombings that occurred in Paris in the fall of 1986 are a good example of this type of attack.

When a specific individual target is selected, persons around that target may also be injured or killed. The terrorists who kidnapped James Dozier struck his wife, and in other cases family members or coworkers of the victim have been beaten up or tied up. If the person targeted has a protective detail (bodyguards), then they are usually killed. In the case of the Aldo Moro kidnapping, the driver and all four bodyguards were killed immediately after the terrorists managed to stop both Moro's vehicle and the chase vehicle following him. In that incident, the Brigate Rosse later murdered Aldo Moro, their victim, when the government refused to respond to their demands.[1]

Innocent people may also be killed when the attack is directed toward a specific group. When the Abu Nidal terrorists attacked the Rome and Vienna airports, they concentrated their attack around the El Al Israeli Airline counters, but many of the killed or injured were citizens of other countries who were unfortunately caught in the fields of fire.

PLANNING PERSONNEL SECURITY

As with all other components of your terrorism counteraction plan, personnel security begins with a review of your threat assessment. Use the assessment to identify the types of targets that have been attacked and the tactics used, then identify the potential targets within your organization. Suppose, for example, you are a military unit stationed in a country where terrorists have been shooting at persons in U.S. military uniforms. This information must be passed on to all personnel, and appropriate counteractions should be considered, such as restricting activities off the installation or encouraging personnel not to wear uniforms or other obvious clothing off base. If you are an industrial organization with personnel working in areas where there have been attacks on private sector executives with smaller companies, then measures must be taken to identify and reduce the risk to those personnel in your organization who fit the at-risk profile.

Your initial step will be to develop a list of personnel who have any degree of risk. You may develop an A list of individuals in a high-risk category due to their position or rank, and a B list of personnel at a lower level of risk. But don't neglect your other employees. Everyone in your organization should be alert to terrorist intelligence collection methods and know to whom they should report suspicious activities,[2] and those traveling internationally could benefit from a briefing on how to travel safely (see page 131). The most important countermeasure is a good awareness and education program that is designed to provide information to individuals based on their level of risk.

Monitor all press releases and other media coverage of personnel within the organization. Remember that terrorists get most of their intelligence information from open-source publications; a seemingly innocent article on a key employee may provide the basis for a target selection, especially if the article includes a picture of the person and personal information. Think like a terrorist! Read each of these articles from their perspective.

Would you select this person as a target and, if so, how would you plan the attack?

Having identified the potential targets within your organization, you can now begin to develop countermeasures. The next step is to conduct a physical survey and an operations security survey. The physical survey of the areas where these people live and work will help you to identify measures that can be taken to improve physical security and access control, and to "harden" these areas. The operations security survey will assist you in identifying the information a terrorist would need to target or plan an attack against these people, and developing appropriate countermeasures to prevent them from getting that information. The operations security survey will also disclose predictable behaviors or patterns and help you to change these before they are identified by a terrorist intelligence cell. In one case, an operations security survey of a Secretary in the United States government identified the fact that his driver kept a battery-operated television in the trunk of the vehicle. While his boss attended meetings and receptions, the driver would put the TV in the front seat and catch up on his favorite soap operas. When he was notified by radio that the Secretary was about to leave a meeting, he would put the TV back in the trunk and drive around to the entrance to pick up his boss. This predictable behavior could have been used by a terrorist to determine when the Secretary was about to emerge from the building in order to time an attack.

If you are responsible for protecting high-risk personnel, you may want to assign a personal security or protective detail (bodyguards) to that person. (A person who is considered at risk, and who has a detail assigned, is referred to as the "principal.") In all cases personnel assigned to this detail should be highly trained and have the appropriate security clearances for this assignment. You may also have to train additional personnel for this function to enable you to handle dignitaries who may be at risk while they are visiting your facilities. Although most political and military principals have their own security details, you may on occasion be tasked with providing protection for a lower-ranking dignitary or an industrial figure who does not have a permanent protective detail. You may also find yourself suddenly asked to provide a detail to someone within your organization because of a drastic change in the risk level of that person. The point is, be sure you have identified and trained your personal security details *before* they are needed. If you do not have the assets available to provide this protection, then your terrorism counteraction plan should include the contacts (for example, an interagency or a contract security service) to call upon when they are needed.

The personnel protection section of your terrorism counteraction plan will also include the actions you will take in response to any attack involving your personnel. You must have plans to protect the high-risk principals not involved in the initial attack and the families of all high-risk personnel, including those initially targeted. Plan to move these people immediately to a secure area and keep them there until the threat has passed. Also, be sure your plan identifies the lead agency responsible for coordinating the response to the action. Any terrorist action in the United States or its possessions, with the exception of an aviation incident, is the responsibility of the Federal Bureau of Investigation, and they should be notified immediately. If the action occurs outside of the United States, contact the local police and the nearest U.S. consulate or embassy. Of course, your plan will also require notification along the command and communication channels within your organization.

If possible, you should develop a set of crisis management files on all high-risk personnel and location files on areas where an incident may take place. Files on personnel include personal data; an example of this file is included as Appendix E. Information on these individuals will prove invaluable if they are taken hostage or kidnapped. Location files consist of the floor plans and interior and exterior photographs of areas where an incident is most likely to occur, such as the executive office area or the homes of high-risk personnel. If a hostage situation occurs, the tactical response forces will be in a much better position to respond if they know the internal layout of the building and have pictures of the area where a hostage rescue assault may be necessary.

AWARENESS AND EDUCATION

Sir Geoffrey Jackson, the British ambassador who was held captive by the Tupamaros (a terrorist organization active in Uruguay during the 1970s) for eight months in a cell six feet long by two feet wide, said afterward that he should have known something was wrong.[3] Sir Geoffrey had observed the Tupamaro intelligence collection cell as they conducted their surveillance of him, but even though he was in a high-threat environment, he didn't tell anyone. Other terrorist kidnap victims also have reported that they felt something was wrong before they were taken captive.

Actually what happens is simple. As you go about your daily routine, your subconscious develops a series of mental maps. Think about how you drive to work. You don't really have to think about the trip at all, and you sometimes experience what is referred to as "highway hypnosis"—you drive to your destination thinking about something else and suddenly realize that you have arrived. But what happens if you encounter something out of the ordinary along the way, such as an unfamiliar van or people taking photographs of your house or office? At the conscious level you may be thinking about a meeting planned for that day, and you may not even be aware of the van or the people. But subconsciously your cognitive map has been disrupted because "something is just not right," and this is converted to a feeling of anxiety. People who are at risk must understand this process. They need to know that if they feel something is wrong, no matter how vague that feeling may be, they must tell someone. You can then set up a countersurveillance plan and, when necessary, provide additional security for the principal until the threat has been neutralized.

Getting the principal to assist in his or her own protection is often the most difficult aspect of providing personnel protection. Some people have an "it will never happen to me" attitude, or they refuse to acknowledge that these types of events occur at all. This is one reason that the principal's family and coworkers should also be made aware of the threat and educated to respond appropriately. These people may observe obvious activities that indicate an intelligence cell in operation or even an impending attack and, if they know what to look for and how to respond, they may be able to prevent that action.

The daughter of a European general who had been selected for assassination by a leftist group answered the telephone three times in one day, responding to questions regarding her father. The first two times, a woman called, asking if her father was home; the daughter answered that he was not but told the woman when he was expected. On the third call the woman asked if the general was home, and when the daughter said yes, the caller hung up. A short time later there was a knock at the front door. When the daughter answered, a woman asked if she could speak to the general. The general came to the door, and after the woman verified that he was the right person, she moved aside. A man with an automatic weapon then stepped out from behind the bushes and assassinated the general. If his daughter had known how to recognize and respond to the situation, the man might still be alive.

Individuals who are at risk must be willing to take some responsibility for their own protection. As part of your awareness and education program, you should provide people in the organization with checklists to help them evaluate and improve the basic security at their workplace and at home. Examples of these checklists are included in Appendix F.

When providing awareness and education for the family and staff of principals, design your awareness training for several different levels and gear your presentation accordingly. The principal, spouse, and adult staff members may get the full treatment, including photographs or movies of terrorist attacks that graphically display the death and destruction that can result. This briefing may also include a detailed discussion of the current threat. However, you would not go into the same graphic detail when briefing younger members of the household. Younger family members should learn basic crime prevention techniques, such as, don't open the door unless you know who is on the other side, don't accept rides with strangers, tell your parents immediately if you see anyone suspicious in the neighborhood or if an unknown person telephones. The Overseas Advisory Council of the U.S. Department of State has developed an excellent movie that is available to private corporations for briefing children who are going to live outside of the United States. Other visual aids are available from a variety of commercial sources (see Appendix B).

Your education process should stress incident prevention. People who are at risk, from the highest executive to the lowest-level person in the organization, should have some awareness of terrorist surveillance techniques and should know how to respond if they suspect that they or the people around them are being surveilled. They also need to understand the basics of good personnel security, including such elementary considerations as maintaining a low profile, varying travel routes, and treating travel itineraries as restricted information.

They should understand how surveillance is conducted and know how to react if they think they are being watched. Since many terrorists are highly trained professionals, the best thing a person can do if he thinks he is being surveilled is to contact law enforcement or security officials as quickly as possible. To prepare people in your organization to deal with this problem, you should provide them with information on the three types of surveillance used by terrorists—foot surveillance, vehicle surveillance, and fixed surveillance.[4]

Foot surveillance. This may involve two or more people from the intelligence cell. Since trained surveillants may change their clothing during a surveillance, the principal should try to note physical characteristics and the way the people walk; he should try also to identify their shoes, since these are not usually changed with the rest of the clothing.

Some basics in responding to this type of surveillance include:

DON'T

• Start looking over your shoulder or doubling back.
• Look back too often or too quickly.
• Jump on and off elevators.
• Run in one door of a building and out another.

DO

• Note the characteristics of the surveillant.
• Look back occasionally when you have a reason for doing so.
• Move away from the street window if you enter a restaurant or lounge.
• Contact the police if you feel you are in danger.

Vehicle surveillance. In spite of what the "Magnum P.I." television series would have you believe, most vehicle surveillance is not conducted by a guy driving a red Ferrari. A professional surveillant will drive a vehicle that blends into the local surroundings. The only modification to the vehicle may be that the inside light will not go on when the door is opened so that the persons conducting the surveillance can enter or leave the vehicle at night without being detected. As with foot surveillance, more than one person, and possibly more than one vehicle, will be used. If you park your vehicle and walk, one of the surveillants will exit their vehicle and follow you while the other parks near your car. Since the object of surveillance is usually to identify a predictable daily pattern, you will be surveilled for several days; if an attack is to occur it will take place within the area where the surveillance took place, such as the routes you use driving to and from work.

Some of the basic do's and don'ts in responding to vehicle surveillance are:

DON'T

- Engage in evasive driving techniques unless you have been trained to do so and have clear evidence of an immediate threat.
- Keep looking over your shoulder or attempt to play cat and mouse with the other car.

DO

- Look for suspicious cars to your front as well as in the rear. You may already be in the trap!
- Try to get a complete description of the vehicle following you and put it in writing.
- Get the license number of the vehicle if possible, but remember that license plates are easily changed.
- If possible, get a description of the people in the vehicle, but don't put yourself at risk to do this.

Fixed surveillance. Most surveillance is conducted from a fixed position over a period of time. The intelligence cell will set up near your home or office and watch these locations for several days, noting when you arrive and leave, what vendors come and go, and other predictable activities. They also will conduct an extensive photo intelligence collection effort during the surveillance. Principals and the people around them should be alert to fixed surveillance teams, especially if they are taking pictures, and they should know how to respond to this threat. These teams may rent an office or apartment near their target but, more often, this surveillance will be conducted from a stationary automobile or van.

DON'T

- Approach the surveillant's position.
- Act as though you are suspicious.
- Stare at the surveillant.

DO

- Take photographs of the surveillant if you can do so discreetly.
- Note descriptions of the individuals.

- Watch to see if they are taking photographs or making notes.
- Look for other surveillants in the area. They may be using several positions.
- Report this activity to the police or your security personnel immediately.

Stress to the people in your organization that individuals assigned to a terrorist intelligence collection cell are trained and committed professionals. Your people should not try to outfox them at their own game, and they should avoid letting the cell know they have been detected, since the reaction may be to kill the person who has spotted them. The only appropriate response if a principal feels he or she is being surveilled is to get to a safe area and notify the police or your security staff.

VICTIM SURVIVAL TRAINING

Another important topic in your education program is victim survival training. (But make sure the emphasis of your program is on prevention so that the training will, hopefully, never be needed.) This training includes survival as a victim during an armed attack, a bombing, a kidnapping, or a hostage-taking. From a prevention perspective, it should also include training in letter and package bomb detection.

If you are trapped during an attack, such as the one the Abu Nidal Group conducted at the airports in Rome and Vienna, the only thing you can do is dive for cover and stay there. Astute travelers in today's world should always be alert as to where they will seek cover if something happens while they are in a line, in a waiting area, or in a public facility such as a restaurant. If an attack does take place, take cover and stay there until the police tell you to move. Innocent victims have been killed because they jumped up during or immediately after an attack and were shot by police who couldn't tell at that point if they were victims or terrorists. Stress repeatedly to your people that they are to stay under cover until told to move by a police officer or security official.

A victim who is injured in a bombing should usually stay in place and wait for help to arrive. However, if the person is not injured, or injured but able to move, it may be best to move out of the immediate area in case the terrorists have planted secondary explosives. Look for any other packages or containers that may hide a secondary device and stay clear of the areas near them.

Survival as a kidnap victim or hostage depends mostly on the individual's maturity and common sense, but there are some techniques to be aware of.[5]

- Be a role model. Try to remain calm and in control so your captors will do the same.
- Be courteous and polite to the terrorists. This is not a time for arguments or belligerence.
- Build human relationships with your captors. Identify those terrorists with whom you can discuss families or other neutral issues.
- Talk in a normal voice. This is part of your serving as the role model.
- Do not complain. Appear to be cooperative and accepting of your situation.
- Don't deliberately turn your back on a terrorist, especially the leader.
- Do not refuse any favors offered by the terrorists. These include offers of food, beverages, and tobacco.
- Manage yourself. Make do with what you have available to maintain your personal hygiene, and exercise regularly if you can.
- Manage your time. Try to establish a regular routine. Keep your mind occupied.
- Manage your environment. Your daily routine should include housekeeping chores to whatever extent they are possible.
- Remember that negotiations and rescue efforts are underway, but do not expect an early release.
- Always be alert for an opportunity to escape or to a possible rescue effort by authorities. If a rescue effort does take place, it is usually best to "hit the floor" and wait for the security forces to identify you. Any sudden movement by a victim during a tactical rescue operation could result in that person being mistaken for a terrorist and, as a result, being killed.
- Don't hesitate to answer neutral questions that will not adversely affect your situation as a victim. Avoid discussions of religion or ideologies.
- Obey all of the terrorists' orders or commands.

The use of letter or package bombs seems to run in cycles. There will be a period of several years when they are seldom used by terrorists, then there will be brief periods when a number of them are discovered. Principals and the people around them must know what to watch for and how to react if they receive a suspect device. Unfortunately, even when they receive this education it is not always taken seriously.

Several years ago the president of a major corporation was sent a package that had all the indications of being a bomb, but, in spite of the training he had received, he opened the package and was badly injured. Several months later an unmarked Christmas package arrived in the mail at a small police department in Tennessee. The officers opened the package and found a lamp, but no card or message. Thinking it was a present from some anonymous admirer in the community, they plugged in the lamp only to find that it was a pipe bomb set for electrical detonation. Both officers were injured but survived; the "anonymous admirer" was never caught. In both of these cases the people involved knew better, but they still became victims of a bomb sent through the mail.

There are several basic indicators of letter and package bombs that people in your organization should be aware of.[6]

Weight

- Unevenly distributed.
- Heavier than usual for its size.
- Heavier than usual for its class of mail.

Thickness

- For medium-sized envelopes, the thickness of a small book.
- Not uniform or with bulges.
- For large envelopes, bulkiness and an inch or more of thickness.

Address

- No return address.
- Poorly typed, handwritten, or hand printed.
- Incorrect title for the executive to whom it is addressed.
- Addressed to a high-ranking executive by title or department.

Rigidity

• Greater than normal, particularly along its center length.

Stamps

• More than enough postage to insure that it reaches its destination.

Postmark

• Foreign.
• From an unusual city or town.

Writing

• Foreign writing style.
• Misspelled words.
• Marked air mail, registered, certified, or special delivery.

Envelope

• Peculiar odor.
• Excessive sealing material.
• Oil stains.
• Springiness.
• Wires, string, or foil sticking out or attached.
• Ink stains.

If someone in your organization receives a suspect package, either at work or at home, they should put the package down gently, clear the area, and call security or law enforcement. Many of the devices being manufactured today are highly sophisticated and include antitampering switches and other special detonating characteristics. In all cases, suspect devices and obvious bombs should be handled only by expert demolition personnel.

PROTECTIVE DETAILS

Personnel assigned to protective details (bodyguards) are a special breed. They must act against all of their self-preservation instincts and learn to protect the principal first, even if that means they are endangering themselves. These individuals must be physically fit to endure the hectic schedule they usually keep, and they must be mentally prepared for the stress of being constantly vigilant and prepared to respond to any threat. They are usually highly skilled in the use of weapons and the martial arts. In addition to being fit and skilled, they must also be trained specifically for this type of duty.

Protective details have three primary missions. First, they are responsible for preventing the assassination or intentional injury of the principal they are assigned to protect. Next, they must prevent an unintentional injury to this person. Finally, they are responsible for the prevention of an embarrassment involving the principal. Embarrassments may include eggs thrown at the principal or having him fall when getting out of a vehicle.

A principal who is assigned a protective detail must know how to work with that detail. It may be difficult for a principal who is used to being in charge to relinquish that authority to a security or law enforcement person when a threat occurs. All of a sudden he is expected to take orders rather than give them, and to respond to those orders instantaneously. He may find himself being pushed into a vehicle or to the ground as the detail protects him from the immediate threat. For the protective detail to be effective, the principal must be willing to work with them and to accept the importance of their role.

In most cases the principal should not be armed. Most higher-ranking officials do not have the time to maintain proficiency with weapons, and even if the person is an excellent marksman he has not been trained in the use of deadly force in these types of situations. Besides, it is the duty of the protective detail to remove the principal from the area where the threat or attack is occurring, not to stay and shoot it out with the adversary.

Protective details receive their greatest challenge when the principal attends a special event such as a football game or an open reception, or when the person is giving a speech to a large audience. Even the most skilled protective detail cannot prevent an incident if the principal insists on exposing himself, as was proved during the attempted assassinations of President Reagan and Pope John Paul. The details also need to know how to go mobile with the principal—from driving from one location to another, to international travel via private or commercial aircraft. Once again, it is imperative that all personnel assigned to protective details be trained and mentally and physically prepared for that assignment.

SECURITY WHILE TRAVELING

You don't usually read about the pickpockets that work the Paris subways or the purse snatchers in New York, but when a terrorist incident occurs you can be assured of hearing all the gory details. Although the probability of becoming a victim during a terrorist incident is extremely small, that probability can be reduced even further by using common sense and some of the techniques and approaches that follow.

The United States Department of State has established several offices that can assist U.S. citizens traveling abroad and U.S. businesses operating overseas. The department can provide information on different countries, and assist citizens who experience problems while out of the country; they have also established a threat analysis division and overseas security advisory council.

Overseas Security Support Division. This office provides security briefings to corporate directors of security, business executives, and other travelers with similar needs. They can provide information on specific regions and countries and introduce you to the department's Regional Security Officer Network.

Citizens Emergency Center. The center is manned twenty-four hours a day and can provide information on travel advisories, visa and other travel requirements, civil disturbances, and even information on available hotel space in major cities around the world. It can also serve as the initial point of contact for a U.S. citizen who experiences problems while traveling overseas, although the center will usually refer you to the nearest U.S. embassy or consulate.

Threat Analysis Division. This division conducts threat analyses that are made available to U.S. citizens and businesses that have established their bona fides with the agency.

The Overseas Advisory Council. The council is a joint venture between the Department of State and the private business sector in the United States. It coordinates joint efforts involving the department and the representatives appointed by the private sector, and it recommends policies and programs to address the needs that are identified as a result of this effort.

The department also has pamphlets and videotapes on traveling safely and it provides speakers and conducts periodic conferences. For more information on any of these services, contact the Bureau of Public Affairs, U.S. Department of State, Washington, D.C. 20520.

Before traveling to another country, there are several basic questions that you should seek answers to.

1. What is the current feeling in the countries where you will be traveling regarding your nationality, race, sex, and religion?
2. Has your organization received any threatening letters or telephone calls in those countries?
3. Is crime a problem in those countries? If so, who are the victims?
4. Have there been any acts of violence against your organization's personnel or other interests?
5. Have other organizations been the victims of recent violence?
6. Are there any groups in those countries who object to your organization's business or policies?
7. Have hostile references been made to your organization in the local media in those countries?
8. Has anyone in your organization had contact with opposition officials in those countries?

If you find yourself answering yes to any of these questions, then you should be prepared to restrict yourself to secure areas and safe activities as much as possible while you are traveling. Maintaining a low profile, staying only in major hotels, and establishing contact with the nearest U.S. consulate are all requisites in this situation.

When you arrive in an area, make sure you know how to contact the local police, the nearest U.S. consulate, and the security personnel in the hotel where you are staying. Also, have someone at home who knows your travel itinerary and expects to be contacted by you at predesignated times during your trip. You should have a predetermined code to let that person know that you are having problems when you call home. For example, you could ask how the dog is doing when you really don't have a dog. This signal would let that person know that you may be a hostage or are having other problems that you cannot talk about openly on the telephone. Remember that in some countries it is common practice for the government-owned telephone system to listen in on certain overseas calls, and that calls made by U.S. citizens traveling on business are often targeted for this type of surveillance.

Before you leave home, make copies of your passport, driver's license, and other identification, and your travelers' checks. Leave one set of these copies with your contact at home and carry another set with you in a suitcase or container other than the one in which you carry the originals. You will need this information if your passport, travelers' checks, or other papers are lost or stolen. Passports, especially United States passports, are valuable commodities on the black market, and stolen passports and other identification papers are routinely used by terrorists while traveling internationally.

The chances of a traveler being specifically targeted by terrorists are small because of the surveillance and planning that precede most terrorist events. However, you could find yourself as a random victim as a result of being in the wrong place at the wrong time. Or you may be selected as a victim because you are a U.S. citizen and the terrorists are targeting that category of victims. The Department of State in a publication entitled "A Safe Trip Abroad" provides some excellent ideas for decreasing your chance of becoming a victim. Some of the recommendations provided by the Department of State include:

- Schedule direct flights if possible and avoid stops in high-risk areas or airports. Consider all of your options for traveling, such as trains.
- Be aware of what you discuss with strangers and what could be overheard by others.
- Try to minimize the time spent in public, nonsecured areas in airports. Move quickly from the counter to a secured area during check in, and on arrival leave the airport as soon as possible.
- Avoid luggage tags, dress, and behavior that may identify you as an American. Leave sweatshirts and clothing with obvious U.S. logos at home.
- Keep an eye out for suspicious abandoned packages or briefcases. Report them to airport security or other authorities and leave the area. *Never* touch or attempt to move a suspect package or briefcase.
- Avoid obvious terrorist targets such as places where Americans are known to congregate.

If you must travel to a high-risk area, the Department of State has some additional considerations. A high-risk area is anyplace that has a recent history of terrorist activities or a location where there are strong anti-American feelings at the present time.

- Discuss with your family what they would do in case of an emergency, in addition to making sure that your affairs are in order before leaving home.
- Register with the U.S. embassy upon arrival.
- Remain friendly, but be cautious about discussing personal matters including your business and itinerary.
- Don't leave personal or business papers in your hotel room.
- Watch for people following you or "loiterers" observing your comings and goings.
- Locate and keep a mental note of safe havens, such as police stations, hotels, and hospitals.
- Let someone else know what your travel plans are. Keep them informed if you make any changes.
- Avoid predictable times and routes of travel and report any suspicious activities to the local police and the nearest U.S. embassy or consulate.
- Select your taxicabs at random; don't take a cab that is not clearly identified as a taxi. Compare the face of the driver with the one posted on his license.
- If possible, travel with others (preferably people who are not high-risk targets).
- Be sure of the identity of visitors before opening the door of your hotel room. Don't meet strangers at unknown or remote locations.
- Refuse unexpected packages.
- Formulate a plan of action that you will follow if a bomb explodes or if there is gunfire nearby.
- Check for loose wires and suspicious activities pertaining to your car.
- Be sure your vehicle is in good operating condition in case you need to resort to high-speed or evasive driving.
- Drive with the windows closed in crowded areas. Bombs can be thrown into the car through open windows.
- If you are ever in a situation where someone starts shooting, drop to the floor or get down as low as possible and don't move until the danger has passed. Do not attempt to help rescuers and do not pick up a weapon. If possible shield yourself behind or under a solid object. If you must move, crawl on your stomach.

If you are traveling to a low-intensity conflict (LIC) area, there are even more special considerations to be aware of. A LIC area is a location where a conflict less than all-out war is occurring. It includes regions experiencing a large number of terrorist incidents, and it usually involves conflicts between rival factions such as the problems experienced in El Salvador or Lebanon in the 1980s. Civilian personnel may have to travel to these areas on business that can be conducted neither elsewhere nor by telephone or other communication. Law enforcement officials, usually from federal agencies, are assigned to some of these areas to assist the local police or security forces or to conduct investigations of crimes that involved American citizens. Military personnel are assigned in support of the local forces, to conduct training missions or as part of a multinational peacekeeping force. Whether you are traveling to a low-intensity conflict area as an individual or as a small group or unit, certain preventive measures should be practiced. The considerations listed here were developed during a joint project conducted by the U.S. Marines and the U.S. Army following the incident at the Marine Landing Team barracks in 1983.

Predeployment. Before you leave, assess and identify the threat that exists along your route of travel and at your final destination. Military units will be required to develop a threat statement that details this assessment; law enforcement and private sector travelers would also benefit from this activity. Compare your mission or purpose in the LIC area with the threat statement, and plan to maintain the lowest possible profile while en route and at your destination.

Talk to someone who knows the area where you will be traveling, and if you are being deployed as a small unit or group, consider augmenting the group with a specialist on that area, a linguist who speaks the local languages, a communications expert, an explosives expert, security personnel, and medical personnel. If you do not have access to people with these areas of expertise, contact the U.S. Department of State before you leave. They may be able to advise you as to what assistance is available within the country.

Make sure that everyone traveling to the LIC area is thoroughly briefed on the threat and that they have received training in personal protection. This training should include information on how to decrease the probability of becoming a victim and how to survive as a kidnap victim or hostage (see previous discussion).

Deployment. The most vulnerable phase of a trip to a LIC area is your movement to and immediate arrival there. If you are moving as a small group or unit, you will need to have established intelligence sources at all key points along the way, and you need to monitor changes in conditions that occur while you are en route. The most vulnerable points in a small unit deployment are:

- Route to the port of embarkation.
- The port itself.
- Transportation used to move the unit.
- Port of arrival.
- Route to your final destination.

These are the points at which you must establish liaison with local law enforcement or security agencies and develop a reliable and dynamic intelligence capability before the unit begins to move. These are also the areas that should be secured before the unit arrives, and security must be maintained the entire time the unit is at these points.

Assess the political climate at your destination and try not to arrive at a time when conflicts are most likely to occur. These include during elections and religious holidays, or during racial or ethnic strife or major demonstrations.

Employment. Once you arrive at your destination, reevaluate and revise your threat statement. If you are a private sector traveler without law enforcement or military support, be sure to contact the nearest U.S. embassy or consulate where the security officer may be able to brief you on the current situation.

Since you are traveling in an area of extreme risk, consider all of the antiterrorism measures we have discussed, including the development of an effective operations security, personnel security, and physical security program. If your organization maintains an ongoing presence in that area (for example, an office, industrial plant, or warehouse), these measures will be developed and implemented by your local security personnel.

And don't forget the need for good communications security. Some corporate travelers have tried to address this need by using portable scramblers on the telephone, only to find that their call gets mysteriously cut off if it cannot be monitored. Others have used a scrambler, ignoring the fact that there may be a listening device in the room recording their side of the conversation before it is scrambled. Unless you have access to secure government communication channels, there is no such thing as total security, and even those channels are compromised occasionally by hostile intelligence agencies. The point is, don't say something that is offensive or sensitive unless you are communicating face-to-face in a secured area or someplace where there is a limited possibility of being monitored or overheard.

Your level of vigilance must remain constant the entire time you are in the LIC area. Be sure also that you monitor and respond appropriately to any changes that take place in the environment around you. If an incident such as the U.S. bombing of Libya takes place after you are in country, an anti-American backlash could occur that would place you in significant danger. Again, if you have a question regarding the local situation and your safety or security, contact the nearest U.S. embassy or consulate.

A checklist of ideas to help you reduce the risk of becoming a terrorist victim while traveling is included in Appendix G. This checklist was originally published by the International Association of Bomb Technicians and Investigators in cooperation with Lockheed Missiles and Space Company, Inc.

Remember that all security awareness and training should be updated and reiterated on a regular basis. Executives who have received training in the past but are now about to be posted to an overseas position need to receive additional briefings on how to reside safely in their new environment. And all persons who are at risk and the people around them (family members and staff) should receive updated briefings on a regular basis. In many cases this is done annually. These briefings include an updated threat assessment, review of any incidents that may have occurred or case studies that have been prepared since the last briefing, a reminder of the basic security measures each person is expected to follow, and the results of physical and operations security surveys that have been conducted.

IMPLEMENTATION CHECKLIST

1. Identify potential victims by category and prepare your A and B lists of possible targets. Categories include:
   a. Specifically selected victims.
   b. Targeted groups of victims.
   c. Personnel who may be involved in a random attack.
2. Planning your antiterrorism personnel security.
   a. Identify high-risk personnel.
   b. Develop your countermeasures.
   c. Harden targets where possible.
   d. Prepare your crisis management and location files.
3. Awareness and education program.
   a. Emphasize the current threat according to your threat assessment and statement.
   b. Stress prevention aspects.
   c. Include information on:
      (1) Foot surveillance.
      (2) Vehicle surveillance.
      (3) Fixed surveillance.
4. Victim survival training should include:
   a. Attacks by terrorists.
   b. Bombings.
   c. Kidnap or hostage situations.
   d. Letter and package bomb recognition.
5. Regarding protective details.
   a. Select personnel for these details and insure that they receive the proper training.
   b. Brief principals on how to work with their assigned details.
6. Security while traveling.
   a. To help you evaluate the threat:
      (1) Contact the U.S. Department of State for current information and periodical updates.
      (2) Review the DOs and DON'Ts listed in this chapter.
   b. When preparing to travel in low-intensity conflict areas, plan separately for each phase.
      (1) Predeployment.
      (2) Deployment.
      (3) Employment.

CHAPTER EIGHT

Physical Security and Antiterrorism

SCENARIO

"It's like he just disappeared off the face of the earth. We have no idea what happened to him." Dave Nelson was telling Fox that the FBI had lost contact with its informant at the APP compound. "The last message we received was that Pardue was planning something big, probably for Armed Forces Day."

"Great," Fox responded. "And we think that the Citizens Against Chemical Warfare have planned their demonstration for that day too. If we're lucky, maybe the two of them will just meet and fight it out. We could go in afterward, pick up the bodies, and make our arrests."

"Fat chance. Anyway, we have one final entry from Pardue's journal that our guy was able to get to us before he disappeared. Take a look."

Charlie began reading Jack Pardue's words: "Soon we will strike at the heart of ZOG, hitting from all sides at once. There will be casualties among the race traitors and mongrels of ZOG, and there will be martyrs among the soldiers of the Aryan Peoples Party. The world will know that we are committed to our cause." The journal entry ended.

Charlie and Dave walked down the hall to the conference room. The TMC was about to meet to review the physical security needs of the high-threat targets in the community. Charlie hoped they could harden those targets before Armed Forces Day. Dave wished he could share the journal entry with the others on the committee, but he still hadn't received clearance to show it to anyone other than Fox or Chief Casey.

Lieutenant Colonel Marsh began the discussion. "We've found that if you start talking to people about antiterrorism, they just think you're an alarmist. It seems that the best way to get cooperation is to talk about crime prevention and then work into physical security and target hardening from a terrorism counteraction perspective. We should identify our immediate needs and then also prepare a list of short- and long-range plans to improve the physical security at potential targets.

"Take this building," Marsh continued. "I noticed when I walked in here that I could go anywhere in the city hall part of the building without being challenged. It's only when I get to this floor with the police department that anyone knows I'm here. This building would be an easy target."

"Tell that to the mayor," Fox grumbled. He had tried to improve the security of the building for the past several weeks but had run into resistance from Mayor Wilson, who felt that since city hall was supposed to belong to the people, it was wrong to turn it into a fortress.

Marsh ignored Fox's comment. "Here are some suggestions. Let's try to improve access control at all potential targets and make sure that our parking areas, wherever official vehicles are parked, are secured. They should be well lighted and patrolled on a regular basis. But keep in mind, too, that all of our physical security should be tied into our operations security plans. Let's not become predictable.

"We also need to organize a series of physical security surveys. If each of you will assign an officer or security person to that detail, I'll have our physical security officer train them. Then we'll know where we stand and what—"

"Physical security is important, more important than we may realize." It was Dave Nelson who interrupted. "But let me remind you that Armed Forces Day is just a week away. We need to do something *now,* right now, if our intelligence is correct. Conducting surveys takes time that we may not have."

Fox supported Nelson. "I agree. We may be facing demonstrations from the Citizens Against Chemical Warfare and who knows what from Pardue's group. We need to harden all potential targets now."

"Easier said than done." It was Sara Lyndon's turn. "The federal building is protected by a separate guard service that is not responsible to any of the agencies on this committee, and they think their job is keeping bums from using the rest rooms. They just don't believe there's a threat."

John Filmore was also pessimistic about his situation. "We all know what needs to be done, but I've just been informed that my budget for security at Toten has been cut by 20 percent and that I have to get management approval for any overtime. Right now I have a request in for overtime next weekend during Armed Forces Day, and it may be rejected."

Lieutenant Colonel Marsh refocused the group on the community's physical security needs, suggesting that a number of things could be done without spending money, for example, making sure that open areas around target buildings are clear and that heavy equipment is available in case they had to block off roads. He also suggested that the members of the committee make random physical security inspections on their own to identify immediate needs.

The meeting ended with everyone agreeing that each organization would be responsible for its own physical security. If anyone needed help, Lieutenant Colonel Marsh's physical security officer would be available. The next meeting was scheduled for Wednesday, three days before Armed Forces Day.

The APP intelligence report on Fort Richardson had just been updated. The areas around the laboratories and chemical storage areas had been hardened. The latest in microwave sensors were in place and patrols had been increased but on a random basis. Good OPSEC, thought Jack Pardue.

But the access to the school remained as open as a highway. Culverts under the fence had washed away; there were no detection devices and no visible guards at the school.

Pardue also had received word that all of his bombs were ready. Several suitcase and package bombs were destined for city hall, and a lunch-box bomb would be carried into Toten Industries by an active supporter. The lunch box would be left in the break area just outside the secure area of the plant. All of these bombs would detonate at 9 A.M. on Friday.

Bombs for the police and FBI cars had also been prepared. The police car parking area was lighted and the cars were locked when not in use, so Jack had four bombs equipped with timers and magnetic attachments. They could be slipped under a car and attached to the gas tank. These bombs would also go off at 9 A.M., as the police were responding to the hostage-taking at Fort Richardson.

The bombs destined for the FBI cars were different. His intelligence team had found that the bureau parked its vehicles in the basement of the federal building, which they considered secure. Actually the lighting was poor, and the one guard on duty came around every hour on a predictable schedule. Since the cars were seldom locked, Jack decided to use pressure-sensitive detonators. They would be placed under the seat on the driver's side so that when an agent got into the car and sat down, the bomb would explode. Four of these bombs would be planted.

Jack was well satisfied with the way his plans were shaping up.

James Raskin's plans were ready to be put into action. The rallying point about 100 miles from Pleasantville had been designated, and the three bus drivers had driven the route to the target area several times. The buses would arrive at the front gate of Fort Richardson at exactly 7 A.M. This would be the CACW's first violent demonstration, although most of the participants didn't know that.

* * *

Your physical security program must be an essential element of your antiterrorism planning. Begin with a basic crime prevention approach and build from there. Be creative as you assess and improve your physical security posture by identifying immediate, short-term, and long-term needs and the approaches you will use to meet these needs.

Many facilities already have a crime prevention program that includes periodic surveys. If you have not yet developed your program, contact the crime prevention bureau of your local police department for initial assistance. Once you have this program in place, you are ready to evaluate your physical security from a terrorism counteraction perspective.[1]

A crime prevention program is designed to keep out criminals. Since there are so many easy targets for criminals to choose from, a simple program that makes access difficult, and apprehension a real possibility, will usually cause them to select another target. But terrorists are different than other categories of criminals. They are highly motivated by their cause, and they are usually more highly skilled and better equipped than common criminals. If you are concerned about the threat of terrorism, then your physical security program must go beyond basic crime prevention.[2]

The first step in addressing physical security is to identify high-risk facilities or areas. Some of these are obvious. Chemical weapons storage sites, nuclear materials, and armories are obvious potential targets for terrorists. So are executive office areas, computer facilities, utility transmission lines and pipes, and major communication centers. The threat management committee should identify those sensitive areas among your assets.

Once these areas have been identified, your next step is to develop a physical security plan. If you already have a plan, review it from the perspective of a terrorism counteraction program. Since most plans are developed in response to the threat of more normal criminal acts, you may have to upgrade yours to also address the threat of terrorism. A basic format for a physical security plan is included in Appendix H.[3] Use this format as a model to develop a plan that addresses your specific needs.

THE PLANNING STAGE

The objective of your antiterrorism physical security plan is "target hardening." You want to make it more difficult for the terrorist intelligence cell to gain access to the areas from which they would collect information, and to make it even more difficult for a tactical cell to be assured that it can gain access to your facilities should you be selected as a target. If you prevent the group from gaining the information or the assurance they need to plan an attack, you may increase the risk to the terrorists beyond an acceptable level and they will select an alternative target. However, there are some exceptions to this concept. A target could be selected because an attack is guaranteed to generate the publicity that terrorists seek even if it is not a tactical success. A European left-wing group fired an RPG rocket at a nuclear power generating station knowing that the action would result in little damage and no disruption in service. Although the only damage was a chip in the concrete, the attack made the front pages of newspapers across Europe.

After you have developed your physical security plan, develop a physical security checklist to evaluate your facilities according to that plan. You may need to develop a series of checklists, depending on the number of facilities or buildings you are responsible for protecting. Special checklists should be developed for high-risk locations, and these areas should be inspected more frequently.

If you have never developed or conducted a physical security survey, it would be a good idea to bring in outside assistance to help you. Again, your local law enforcement agency may be able to assist you in accomplishing this objective. There are also numerous professional consultants in this area, but before you contract with an outside consultant make sure you investigate the firm. Front organizations have been used to contract with potential targets for these services, and the contractors then have shared the information they acquired, and the recommendations they made, with the infrastructure supporting the terrorist group. A good source for identifying reputable contractors is the American Society for Industrial Security.

When conducting the survey it is a good idea not to assign people to the areas where they work on a daily basis. When you work in the same area everyday, your senses begin to accommodate to your surroundings. You no longer see the broken latch on the window or other problems because you're around them all the time. If possible, have people from another work area conduct the survey so they will see the environment from a fresh perspective. Plan to have at least two people working together as they survey an area. These survey teams should report the results of their physical security survey and their recommendations to the threat management committee.

The needs identified during the survey should be divided into three categories: those that require immediate action, short-term needs that should be corrected within the next twelve months, and long-term needs that will require more than twelve months to address due to budgetary or other considerations. Immediate needs may include repairing windows and doors, and replacing locks and barriers. Short-term needs can involve installing a new intrusion-detection system or remodeling the reception room to restrict views into other areas of the facility. Long-term projects might involve the erection of expensive perimeter protection systems, building new buildings, or replacing an intrusion-detection system with all new state-of-the-art equipment.

When planning improvements try to take advantage of natural barriers in the area and to use equipment you already have. Culverts and drainage ditches can be strategically placed to prevent a vehicle from approaching across an open field, or they can be placed beside a road so traffic will not be able to go around a barrier that you might place there during a high-threat condition. And you may already have access to the equipment needed to increase security during an emergency or a high-threat period. Trucks, especially dump trucks and tractor trailers, can be used to block entrance routes, driveways, and roads. If the threat is going to persist for a period of time and you are concerned about the possibility of vehicle bombs, a truck load of sand dumped on the road can be an effective, yet temporary, barrier. Identify all the equipment you would need to improve physical security during a high-threat situation and list the equipment, sources, and their use in your physical security and terrorism counteraction operational plans.

BASIC CONSIDERATIONS

Access control is an important consideration when evaluating your physical security needs. Use unannounced inspections and penetration tests to examine the **reality** of who can access what areas at certain times. Many facilities have installed locks on interior doors that require a card or code access to open. But some employees, finding these barriers to be a nuisance, prop open the doors and completely negate the intent of the security. Cleaning crews may arrive at night and prop open all of the doors, which means anyone who can gain access to the building at that time can go wherever he pleases.

Employee access in sensitive installations may be restricted to the immediate work and break areas, whereas vendors, like the soft drink–machine man, may have almost free access. Make sure that your access control plans cover *all* people, including employees, vendors, visitors, and anyone else who may come to your facility.

Consider also the access of vehicles within and near the facility. Routes should be limited, and parking areas clearly labeled and located away from the buildings if possible. Ideally, routes leading up to sensitive facilities or areas will be circuitous, rather than straight, to prevent a suicide terrorist from building up speed and repeating what occurred at the Marine Corps Landing Team barracks.

You also need to control the access of goods and materials coming into the facility. During a high-threat period you should monitor the mail to detect possible package or letter bombs before they get to their targets. All incoming goods should be checked and, as previously discussed, the movement of all vendors should be monitored while they are at your facility. The best way to prevent a bombing from occurring is to make it difficult, if not impossible, to get the bomb to the target area.

Parking areas should be monitored. If a person parks a car in the area and then attempts to leave the facility, they should be identified and questioned. There may be a legitimate reason for their behavior, but they may also be leaving behind a vehicle bomb, like the Red Army Faction bomb that exploded and killed two people in the parking lot at Rhein Mein Air Force Base.

Visitor areas, including your reception area, personnel offices, and display area, should be examined as if you were a terrorist. If I can sit in the reception area and see your main switchboard, then I know where to knock out your communications. If the public rest rooms are "down the hall past the computer room," then I have identified another sensitive area. If I have a visitor's pass that allows me only on the third floor, but the elevator stops at all floors and no one asks me why I'm walking around on a floor other than the one authorized by my pass, then the difference between the security you have on paper and the reality of that security could be fatal.

An example of a security failure: A police department in a high-threat area instituted a visitor pass procedure that restricted visitors to the floor they were authorized to be on, based on the color of the pass. But they also developed a VIP pass that allowed visitors to access all floors; those passes were issued to people who claimed they needed to visit more than one office in the building. A terrorist using a VIP pass managed to carry a bomb into the building in a briefcase, which he left on top of a file cabinet. He turned in his VIP pass and left, and no one asked where his briefcase was. When he entered the facility he had to show his driver's license, but none of the information on the license was recorded, so the department had no leads as to his identity. The bomb exploded, causing considerable damage in the immediate area, but fortunately there were no serious injuries.

Look also at the **labels on parking spaces and buildings.** Are parking spaces for executives designated by name or title? Both make it easy for a terrorist to identify which car he is going to follow or plant a bomb in. Or how about planting a bomb near that parking space and detonating it when the executive arrives at work and is getting out of his car? As obvious as all this sounds, many companies still have identifiable parking spaces, as do some military installations and government agencies. If you visit the FBI academy at Quantico, Virginia, you will find two clearly designated spaces next to the front door—one for the deputy director in charge of the academy and the other for the director of the FBI.

Consider, too, the labels on your buildings and on the maps of your areas. Most maps of military installations show clearly where chemical and petroleum products are stored and the locations of the offices of the commanders as well as their residences. All of these locations are also designated by cute little signs on the front lawn. A few installations even have signs at the entrance that lead people entering the facility directly to the emergency operations center. A terrorist tactical unit really doesn't need much intelligence information to carry out an attack when the route to the target is already laid out. If signs and other designations must be used, it is better to number parking spaces and buildings. There should not be a number "1"; start with two-digit numbers and do not number the spaces consecutively. Five adjoining parking spaces might be numbered 54, 32, 75, 14, and 26. Identify buildings by number, trying not to disclose which buildings house your sensitive offices and facilities.

Use your creativity in planning **barriers around sensitive areas.** Some of these, such as perimeter fencing or high walls, are man-made, whereas others may be natural barriers, such as thorny hedges. One company has started importing a bush with vicious-looking thorns several inches long. The bush grows into an attractive hedge, which, when placed around industrial plants and sensitive installations, becomes a formidable barrier to any adversary. If you are really creative, you can combine man-made and natural barriers to be aesthetically pleasing as well as highly effective. One military installation is planting the thorny bush around strands of concertina wire. When the plants are mature, the installation will have an attractive barrier that will be very difficult to compromise.

There should be a clear zone around each building and around all protective barriers. This is an area where the grass is kept low and there are no bushes or other places for a terrorist or other criminal to hide. These zones should be well lighted at night. All other open areas, including parking lots and walkways, should also be lighted.

If your building adjoins other buildings over which you have no control, find out who is located in those buildings. Make a special effort to identify organizations that are literally on the other side of the wall from your assets. Approach these people in a friendly manner, but make sure you find out who and what they are. The greater the threat, the more important this activity becomes.

Intrusion-detection systems have become highly complex with the development of modern technology. Before you seriously consider purchasing a system or replacing your present system, you should probably consult with an expert in the field, unless you are fortunate enough to have the expertise in-house. If you call on the equipment companies themselves for assistance, make sure you get a proposal and costs from at least three different companies (this should be common practice). Consider using intrusion-detection systems for all sensitive areas, including the homes of high-risk personnel. The dollars invested in these systems and the level of sophistication required will be commensurate with the threat against the facility or building. If you are a licensed or regulated facility, such as a nuclear weapons storage site, then the licensing agency will dictate the minimum requirements that must be met by your system.

Security guards and other personnel assets play an important role in your physical security program. If you hire proprietary guards, be sure to conduct an extensive background investigation on every person and periodically run a new investigation on randomly selected guards. If you are using a contract guard service, you should know what screening procedures they use to hire their personnel. In all cases security guards should be competently trained and receive ongoing training during their employment. Only individuals who are properly trained and qualified should be armed, and these personnel should be required to complete the same annual requalification as most law enforcement officers and military personnel.

Make sure, also, that guards are debriefed at the end of their shift by a competent supervisor. They may see or hear something that doesn't mean much as an isolated piece of information but becomes valuable when pieced together with other data available to your security department.

VALIDATING YOUR PHYSICAL SECURITY

Physical security is both an art and a science. It takes a true artist to identify your physical security needs from a terrorism counteraction perspective and then develop a plan to manage your threat and vulnerability. At the same time it takes a highly skilled technician to determine what devices should be used and how they will be used. As part of the validation process, these systems also need to be monitored, and corrections and modifications made as needed. Because physical security is so complex, you will need someone with the proper expertise to assist you with this part of your terrorism counteraction plan. Make sure the firm or individuals you use have a working knowledge of terrorism counteraction in addition to their physical security expertise. As stated earlier, you can identify potential consultants through the American Society for Industrial Security.

Your **physical security surveys** are a method of validating the effectiveness of your program. If you repeatedly identify the same problems and weaknesses, then your program is not working. Be sure that you update the checklists used for your surveys on a regular basis. Updates should be recommended by the individuals who conduct the surveys and then approved by the entire threat management committee.

Random checks and inspections are also used to test the program. Show up when you are least expected and see if all of your access control measures are being followed. Park an old car in the parking lot for a couple of days and see if anyone notices. Walk your perimeter fence after a heavy rainstorm to see if areas under the fence have been washed away, allowing easy access to your facilities. Inspect clear areas on a regular basis to make sure they really are clear, and periodically conduct these inspections at night to evaluate the effectiveness of your lighting program.

In an earlier chapter we discussed **penetration teams** and their use against high-risk targets. Occasionally you may want to hire a security consultant to attempt to penetrate your physical security. This person may show up at your facility posing as a vendor or job applicant and try to gain access to areas where he or she should not be allowed to go. He could write your public relations or public affairs office asking for maps, biographical information, or other materials that might help him breach your defenses, to see if they are sent to him.

Even the best physical security program and procedures can be breached by someone who has the right expertise and the time required. In fact, physical security is actually measured in terms of penetration time—the time required for an adversary to compromise your physical security using tools that are normally available.

Since you cannot achieve the ultimate objective of absolute security, your physical security program should be designed to accomplish three objectives: first, to make the penetration time long enough that high-risk personnel who may be the target of the attack can escape via another route; second, to allow time for security or law enforcement personnel to arrive at the scene and apprehend or otherwise stop the terrorist before the penetration is completed; and finally, to make it difficult for a terrorist intelligence cell to collect the information they need to effectively plan an attack, or for a tactical cell to enter your facilities with a reasonable expectation of effectively planting a bomb that will not be discovered before it is detonated.

IMPLEMENTATION CHECKLIST

1. If you do not already have a physical security program, start by contacting your local police department or an outside contractor to help you review your basic physical security needs from a crime prevention perspective. Once these needs have been addressed, you may begin looking at physical security from an antiterrorism perspective.
2. Identify high-risk areas and facilities.
3. The antiterrorism physical security planning stage:
   a. Remember the concept of target hardening.
   b. Prepare a physical security plan and survey checklists.
   c. Conduct your physical security surveys.
   d. Identify your physical security needs according to:
      (1) Immediate needs.
      (2) Short-term needs.
      (3) Long-term needs.
4. While planning physical security improvements, remember to consider:
   a. Access control systems.
   b. Vehicle parking.
   c. Visitor and reception areas.
   d. Labels on parking spaces and buildings.
   e. The use of barriers, natural and man-made.
   f. Intrusion-detection systems.
   g. Security guards.
5. Validate your physical security using:
   a. Physical security surveys.
   b. Random inspections.
   c. Penetration teams.

CHAPTER NINE

Responding to a Terrorist Incident

SCENARIO

The threat management committee meeting on Wednesday was solemn. Everyone knew that their antiterrorism program still needed a lot of work, and they also believed that, ready or not, it would be tested on Saturday—Armed Forces Day.

The latest intelligence reported increased activity at the APP compound, although Jack Pardue had not been seen for the past week. It was also known that the Citizens Against Chemical Warfare had rented a number of motel rooms about 100 miles from Pleasantville and expected about 100 members to meet there on Friday. The FBI thought they would plan and rehearse the demonstration at the rallying point on Friday, then ride chartered buses to Fort Richardson on Saturday morning.

The tension at the TMC meeting became evident when Deputy Chief Fox, on orders from Chief Casey, reminded everyone that Casey was the number one law enforcement official in Pleasantville. If anything happened on Saturday, he, Casey, would take charge of the police response. Dave Nelson in turn reminded Fox that all acts of terrorism come under FBI jurisdiction, which meant *his* boss would be in charge.

"They're just a bunch of damn criminals," Fox exploded. "You guys think there's some glory to grab here and you want to be first in line. Just remember, this is our community!"

Other committee members jumped in to quiet the dispute. "This is no time to be arguing among ourselves." Lieutenant Colonel Marsh took charge and tried to calm everyone down. "We have a real threat here. Let's make sure our crisis management team is ready to deal with whatever happens. We can worry about jurisdiction on Saturday morning. I'm sure all of our bosses are going to want to be here and know what's going on."

"You're right. I'm sorry, Dave," Fox responded. "We need to be pulling together."

"Let's define the threat," Nelson said, getting the meeting back on track. "We know we're facing a demonstration at Fort Richardson by the Citizens Against Chemical Warfare. In the past, all of their actions have been non-violent. Let's hope it continues that way. Anything that happens outside of the gate the police department will be responsible for. In fact, I've asked the state highway patrol to provide additional backup personnel and they've agreed. Anything that happens at the boundary of the fence, or inside, is the responsibility of Lieutenant Colonel Marsh's people."

Everyone agreed.

"Now let's examine the APP threat," Nelson suggested. "They are capable of bombings and shootings, but I don't think we have to worry about any hostage-takings. What I'm concerned about is multiple bombings. We better make sure that all potential targets are secured and kept under surveillance beginning at noon on Friday. We also should notify the local hospitals to be prepared for an unusual emergency response on Saturday morning."

Again, everyone agreed.

"The emergency operations center will be in this room," Fox added. "We're setting up extra radios and telephones, and we've located the media center in the auditorium downstairs. All of our officers will be on duty, and the department's tactical teams will be on alert starting at midnight on Friday."

Sara Lyndon reported that BATF would have additional bomb technicians available, and Karen Dall agreed to handle the liaison with the hospitals and the other major emergency response tasks. Lieutenant Colonel Marsh would remain at Fort Richardson, and John Filmore would be on duty at Toten Industries, but each would send a representative to help coordinate activities at the emergency operations center (EOC).

To settle the earlier dispute, everyone agreed that Charlie Fox would be responsible for setting up the EOC and that jurisdictional responsibility would be decided as the events unfolded. Both Chief Casey and the local FBI special agent in charge would be present in the EOC.

The EOC would become operational at noon on Friday with most of the committee members and their representatives actually arriving around 5 A.M. on Saturday. Between noon on Friday and 5 A.M. Saturday, everyone would remain on call. If anything happened before Saturday, the EOC could be fully staffed within thirty minutes. Charlie Fox would sleep down the hall in his office on Friday night.

"Surprise, Charlie." Dave Nelson was on the telephone. "Our demon-strators just left on their buses. We think they're on the way to Fort Rich-ardson."

"But it's only Friday! I thought we had another day." Fox looked at his clock. It was 5:30 A.M. "Meet me at the police station in thirty minutes. I'll telephone Marsh and tell him what's happening."

Fox rolled out of bed and telephoned Lieutenant Colonel Marsh. He debated on whether to call Phil Casey, but decided to wait until he had more information. Maybe this was just a rehearsal and the demonstrators really weren't coming until tomorrow.

As Fox and Nelson arrived in the conference room, the CACW dem-onstrators were just stepping off the buses at Fort Richardson. First reports from officers at the scene indicated that it looked like a peaceful group. Two movie stars and a well-known socialist clergyman were with them. And, of course, the media began arriving at the same time the demon-strators' buses pulled into the parking lot. Fox had just talked to Marsh, who felt they had things under control.

The highway patrol said it would be an hour before their reinforcements could arrive, and Fox had already called in all of his off-duty officers. The EOC was being activated, and all of the police department's tactical units were now on alert and waiting in the police locker room area. The city's public information officer was establishing a media room in the auditorium; Chief Casey was on his way in. Things were going according to plan.

But before the EOC could be activated fully, a call came into the police dispatcher: There had been a shooting at Sheriff Potter's house. It was 7:30 A.M.

The first officers on the scene found the sheriff's body on the front lawn. He had been shot with automatic weapons while on the way to his car. The officer didn't know how many times he had been hit, but his body was almost cut in half. His wife lay in a pool of blood on the front steps. She had heard the shots and come running out of the house, only to be killed along with her husband. The sheriff's teenage son was standing behind his mother when she was shot and was badly wounded himself. He said there were at least three gunmen, all armed with automatic weapons.

From his safe house near Fort Richardson, Jack Pardue was monitoring the action as it unfolded. The diversion had worked. Police were being dispatched to the sheriff's house. But Jack didn't understand all the com-motion at the front gate of the fort. His people were supposed to go in through the fence some distance away from the gate. Jack was also sur-prised by the CACW demonstration, and it was causing him major problems. All of the fort's security personnel were being activated and the entire installation was put on alert status. The school stayed closed and all personnel were encouraged to remain in their quarters.

The APP tactical team did not have contact with Pardue and so had breached the perimeter fence as ordered. They were spotted as they approached the school and were now in a fire-fight with a military police patrol. It wasn't going to be much of a match unless reinforcements for the MPs arrived quickly; Jack's people had better weapons and more ammunition.

What the tactical team didn't know was that Jack had placed radio detonators in their explosive packs. When he heard the shooting from his safe house, he decided to push the button. All five members of the team died instantly, their bodies badly mangled and their souls martyred for the APP. The MPs thought the tactical team members had committed suicide by detonating their own explosives.

The demonstrators at Fort Richardson heard the shooting and the explosions and became confused and frightened. Most of them ran for the buses in the parking lot across from the front gate. The professional agitators among them reacted by shooting BB-coated cherry bombs into the crowd and throwing tear gas canisters at the police and security personnel. The highway patrol reinforcements arrived just in time to start making arrests. The police were determined to regain control of the area.

Fox and Nelson were trying to get everything under control in the EOC. Chief Casey had arrived and wanted a briefing, but too much was happening to take the time.

All of a sudden they heard explosions at the federal building, one block from city hall. The report soon came in that two FBI agents, one of them Dave Nelson's boss, had gotten into their cars at the same time. Both were now dead. The building was sealed off, so agents from BATF could begin a thorough search for more bombs.

It was only 9 o'clock on Friday morning, but Charlie Fox and Dave Nelson felt as though they had already been through a war. Mayor Wilson was in the EOC screaming about the police department not doing its job and the FBI not being any help either. The mayor's shouting was drowned out by the sound of additional explosions. Jack Pardue's timed devices were going off.

The first floor of city hall was devastated. At least four bombs had gone off there. The dead and wounded were everywhere, including the body of Karen Dall. She had just arrived in the building to coordinate the medical response.

Four police cars exploded at the same time. Two were parked in front of city hall and there were no casualties. The other two were being used to respond to the demonstration at Fort Richardson. Two arrested demonstrators had just been placed in the backseat of each car. They were killed, and four police officers were wounded when those bombs went off.

At Toten Industries, four people were taking a break when they noticed a lunch box sitting under the table and no one else around. Remembering the briefing John Filmore had given them on Thursday, they cleared the area just as the lunch box exploded. There was some damage but no injuries. Filmore had decided that if the company wouldn't provide him with the resources needed to improve his security posture, at least he could increase the knowledge and awareness of the plant's employees. Every employee had received a special briefing on how to recognize a suspect device, and they were told to leave the area immediately if they saw anything unusual. Filmore's determination had just saved four lives.

Later that day, when it seemed as though the terror was all over, Charlie Fox tried to figure out what had happened. They had done everything they could and still they weren't able to keep the demonstrators or the terrorists from destroying their community.

Dave Nelson was in shock. He hadn't experienced anything like this since Vietnam.

Mayor Wilson was also upset. He would probably lose the election.

*   *   *

When a terrorist attack occurs, law enforcement and security forces must consider the possibility that the initial attack may be a diversion. They need to immediately secure their primary areas of responsibility and not leave those areas to go to the scene of the incident, unless ordered to do so. An example of what can happen: Terrorists in Rome threw an explosive device over the wall of the British Embassy, where it landed in a fountain. When police from all over the city converged on this area, a lone terrorist in a hotel across from the United States Embassy was able to fire several rockets at the building. With all of the police responding to the incident at the British Embassy, the terrorist could take his time leaving the hotel and make a clean escape. Law enforcement and security personnel must not be drawn away by diversionary tactics.

Your incident response plan must also include provisions for securing sensitive areas and high-risk individuals. In the Rome example described above, the proper response should have been for police near the U.S. Embassy, and other embassies in the city, to *increase* their visible presence and their awareness near those potential targets. Additional security forces should have been sent to other sensitive targets, such as the U.S. Embassy, and key individuals, including all ambassadors and their security officers, should have been notified so that they could activate or increase their personal protection plans and details.

There are three phases you will go through when responding to a terrorist incident.[1] The initial phase is designed to contain and stabilize the situation. The second phase involves the possible transfer of jurisdiction over the incident to the appropriate lead agency. And the third phase is when additional resources are allocated and the incident is resolved.

Phase I. The first response to any terrorist incident is to contain and stabilize the situation while the initial information is confirmed. In fact, you may not know immediately that this is a terrorist incident. A bomb can be planted by a disgruntled employee, a jilted lover, or a criminal psychopath. It may be some time after the device goes off that a terrorist group claims responsibility. In that case the immediate jurisdiction would usually go to the local police; once the incident is identified as a terrorist event (assuming it takes place in the United States) jurisdiction would be transferred to the Federal Bureau of Investigation.

The same transition could occur during a hostage-taking event. Initially it may appear that the hostages were taken by felonious extortionists as part of a criminal event, and the hostage-takers may not be identified as terrorists until several hours later. The jurisdictional situation could be further complicated if for some reason the hostage-takers are in fact criminals but claim to be politically motivated terrorists.

In addition to the initial response to contain, stabilize, and verify the situation, several other steps should be taken during Phase I. These include establishing law and order in the area around the incident, and identifying and activating the appropriate emergency contingency plans.

Phase II. The second phase is when the transfer of jurisdiction actually occurs. The FBI, host country, or other lead agency may request that the law enforcement and security assets initially committed remain in place in support of their jurisdiction and subsequent actions.

During this phase you will also attempt to collect as much intelligence as possible on the situation and all of the people involved. This includes information on the incident area, the hostages or other victims, and the individuals and group responsible.

Phase III. This phase begins when additional law enforcement or military assets are committed to manage the situation. If the incident is a hostage situation, these forces may be tactical. If it is a bombing or kidnapping event, they may be investigative. This phase continues until the incident has been terminated and the post-incident analysis and activities are completed.

When an incident does occur, plan for a long-term or multiple-event situation. If the incident was a bombing, plan for secondary and other additional devices. There may be multiple bombs at several locations, secondary bombs at the initial incident area, or a series of bombs exploded over a period of time, like the wave of terrorist bombings that occurred in Paris in September 1986.

The worst possible scenario you could be confronted with is a long-term terrorist hostage-taking event. It would require more personnel to control this situation than most agencies have readily available, and it would truly test your public affairs and media relations capabilities as the terrorists attempt to manipulate the media reporting on the event.

An attack by terrorists is usually a brief event. They don't intend to engage in a long firefight but prefer to use hit-and-run tactics. An attack against the INTERPOL headquarters in France is a good example: Members of Direct Action threw one hand grenade and sprayed the front of the building with automatic weapons, then jumped into their vehicle and escaped from the scene. Your best reaction to this type of an event is to identify possible escape routes and seal them off as quickly as possible.

PERSONNEL RESPONDING TO THE INCIDENT

Most of the training and other activities conducted in preparation for the response to a terrorist attack is tactical. Major police departments and military installations have tactical units that are trained in special assault procedures, intelligence collection, and the other skills needed to contain, stabilize, and terminate an incident. Departments and installations also have hostage negotiators who apply their craft in an attempt to convince terrorists and other hostage-takers to surrender instead of forcing the tactical response. A highly trained tactical unit will be used to:

- Evacuate innocent people from the incident area.
- Man the inner perimeter of a hostage-taking site.

- Rescue hostages.
- Apprehend hostage-takers and other terrorists.
- Attack with riot control agents.
- Provide countersniper fire.
- Assault the terrorist position.
- Collect intelligence while operating covertly in LIC areas.

It has been suggested by one expert in the field that corporations should band together into consortiums, and each consortium develop its own private sector SWAT team that could be dispatched anywhere in the world if an executive from a member company is kidnapped or taken hostage, or if a company asset is otherwise targeted by a terrorist group.[2] This is a terrible idea! A unit operating independently of any government sponsorship would not have the intelligence needed to carry out those types of operations, and they would most likely interfere with ongoing government actions (tactical, political, or economic negotiations) to end the situation. An action by that type of team would probably result in the death of the hostages, the capture or death of the team members, embarrassment to the country from which the team originated, and a backlash of attacks against the assets of the companies that sponsored them. Tactical responses should be left to law enforcement, military, and other government forces.

Both public and private sector organizations, however, should have an emergency operations or crisis management capability to manage ongoing terrorist activity targeted against them. Ideally the threat management committee would assume this role since its members are most familiar with both your antiterrorism and counterterrorism programs. However, in some situations, such as a military installation that has an established command structure, the committee will act in an advisory capacity, assisting the management or command structure in responding to the event. For our purposes we will refer to this group and the environment in which they operate as the Emergency Operations Center (EOC).

In a military, police, or other government agency, the EOC will actually manage the incident. They will commit tactical forces to the scene, assume responsibility for the intelligence collection and criminal investigation activities that will lead to the apprehension and conviction of the terrorists for their crimes, and form liaisons with other governments or agencies as they are needed to address the threat. In the private sector these corporate teams may not have the ultimate decision-making responsibility, but they do perform an important function. The private sector EOC operates in support of the law enforcement or government emergency operations by providing access to company assets as needed. These assets may include information on the personnel involved and the area where the incident is occurring, assuming it is taking place in a company facility. The company EOC will be responsible for determining if other company operations should resume their normal activities, for deciding if a ransom is going to be paid in kidnap or hostage situations, and for supporting and protecting the families of the victims. In all cases, both public and private sector, the EOC members should be identified and trained long before the first incident occurs. If you are concerned about the threat of terrorism to your organization, part of your counteraction should be the formation and training of the emergency operations center.

The crisis management personnel assigned to the EOC will represent eight basic roles, and they should be supported or augmented by other specialists according to the needs of the situation. The basic team includes the following:

1. *Executive or commander.* This is the individual in charge of all crisis management team activities and decisions. In some cases this person is responsible for managing the entire incident and all of the assets committed, including the tactical teams. In other situations, this individual may be responsible for immediate decisions made within the EOC but may be subordinate to a higher command with respect to other decisions such as committing the tactical forces to an assault.

2. *Assistant commander.* This is the number two person on the CMT. One of this person's key responsibilities is to insure that all available information is shared by all members of the team and that the events are recorded as they occur. Available information should be displayed on chart paper with each person on the team having a separate area and chart pads to work on. Anyone walking into the EOC could then look around the room and know exactly what was happening. It is important that all of the events that occur during a terrorist incident be recorded for use later in all subsequent legal proceedings and to conduct a post-incident analysis. Since every terrorist event is also a legal event (either the terrorists are prosecuted for their crimes, you are sued for overreacting or not reacting properly, or both), it is advantageous for

this person to be an attorney. He can therefore advise the CMT on the legal aspects of their operations and decisions during the time the team is activated.

3. *Law enforcement specialist.* This is the "chief cop" or security person on the CMT. This individual controls the law enforcement or security assets committed to monitoring the incident and co-ordinates whatever assets are in reserve.

4. *Operations specialist.* This counterterrorism operations specialist is the right-hand person to the executive or commander in charge of the CMT. He should be familiar with negotiation processes, tactical responses, and all other aspects of the situation.

5. *Intelligence specialist.* This person receives intelligence from at least three sources during a hostage-taking event, then shares that information with the CMT. He receives information from the incident area, from investigators in the field collecting intelligence on the hostages and the hostage-takers, and from experts who have data on the group responsible. This person is also charged with conducting a terrain analysis of the area where the incident is taking place and with monitoring the weather and any meteorological changes that could affect the situation.

6. *Logistics specialist.* This member of the team will arrange for any special equipment or materials that may be needed, transportation as required, and any other logistical needs. He will provide for the basic human needs of the personnel committed to the inner and outer perimeters of hostage-taking situations, people in the CMT operations center, and all others committed to the response.

7. *Personnel specialist.* This individual works with the law enforcement representative to identify and monitor the use of all personnel committed to the response or held in reserve. He should know where to access additional personnel when needed. He handles all other aspects of the personnel situation: monitoring the amount of overtime pay the agency is accruing; forming liaisons with other agencies for use of their personnel and determining pay, insurance, and other considerations that will result from those liaisons; and working with the logistics specialist to insure that the needs of all personnel are being met.

8. *Public affairs specialist.* Every terrorist event is a media event, and to handle it correctly you will need the advice and assistance

of a media specialist. This individual coordinates all the information released to the press, arranges for and conducts most of the press briefings, assures that the media representatives are housed in a comfortable room away from the operations center, and advises the CMT on what information should be released and how the press and the public will react to that information.

The CMT will be augmented or supported by specialists in other areas, depending on the situation. These additional personnel may include a language or cultural specialist who can advise the CMT on the cultural considerations of the terrorists or the environment where the incident is occurring; an explosives expert who can brief the CMT on the types of devices used and what can be expected as the incident continues; a psychologist who can provide advice with respect to the mind-set and personality of the terrorists and their victims; and engineers who can provide information on the buildings where the incident is taking place, blast effects that could result from the use of explosives, and other technical considerations depending on the discipline of the engineer.

Managing a terrorist event that lasts for any period of time is a demanding and stressful task. For that reason the emergency operations center should be as spacious and comfortable as possible so the team members do not become fatigued or burned out. If the event is going to last for an extended period of time, you will need alternates for the regular team members, and you will need to rotate those alternates through the operations center, with a shift change every eight to twelve hours. The EOC should have secure communications with the incident area and higher headquarters.

As discussed, each of the major functions represented on the CMT should have chart paper and an area to display the information for which they are responsible. The assistant commander will maintain several charts, including a log of all the events as they occur and a list of demands made by the terrorists. The law enforcement and personnel specialists will list the assets that have been committed and the units or people held in reserve. The intelligence specialist will post the information he receives that is relevant to the situation, and the same is done by the operations specialist, who might also list the options that are being considered. The logistics specialist will identify past, present, and future logistical needs and the materials and sources used to address those needs. The public information specialist will list the information provided to the media in past statements and the time of the next anticipated statement.

Anyone walking into the CMT operations center should be able to process visually the information posted and know immediately what is occurring, how the situation has unfolded thus far, what assets have been committed or are otherwise available, and what options are being considered. Since all of this information is readily available, only authorized personnel are allowed into the EOC.

Your response must also outline how you will handle the media representatives. Provide these people with a comfortable room with the electrical and communications outlets they will need. Provide them with appropriate information at regular intervals and make sure that all information released goes through one source—the CMT's public affairs specialist. This will help to minimize the conflicting information that inevitably emerges during any crisis. Make sure, too, that you do not release anything to the media that you are not prepared to see immediately on a special TV news broadcast or in the next edition of the newspaper. When dealing with the media during a crisis, there is no such thing as confidential information or media restraint. Whatever the media learns, with rare exceptions, they use.

If you are responding to a hostage-taking incident, you will have to establish a forward command post. This unit includes personnel assigned to the inner and outer perimeters in the incident area, the hostage-negotiation team, the forward intelligence specialist, and the forward command post commander. The inner perimeter monitors the activities at the incident site and apprehends anyone, hostage or hostage-taker, who attempts to leave the area. The outer perimeter prevents people from entering the area. These may include supporters of the terrorists, friends of the hostages who are attempting to take their own actions, and reporters looking for a story. The negotiators attempt to maintain contact with the terrorists, and all of their communications are monitored by the forward commander and by the CMT.

BOMBINGS AND BOMB THREAT RESPONSES

What will be your first response to a bomb threat at any of the facilities or assets you are responsible for protecting? In some cases the entire area is immediately evacuated, whereas in other situations this is impossible. The key to your response should be based on your prior planning and training of your personnel.

First consider the point at which the bomb threat is received. This is usually via telephone to one of your operators or other employees, so these people need to know what to listen for and what to ask if a threat is received. Appendix I includes bomb threat call sheets that can be used to record the information received during the threat.[3] The person receiving the call should attempt to identify the sex, approximate age, and nationality of the caller, while also getting that person to reveal as much about the device as possible. A caller who cannot explain his own device is probably a hoax, but one who can explain in detail how the device is assembled and how it will detonate must be taken seriously.

When a threat is received, your response should be to dispatch bomb search teams. These are trained employees who know how to look for a suspect device, what to look for, and how to react if they find it. Team members should be employees who work in the search area every day. Waiting for a police officer to arrive and find the device for you is not logical. The officer, who has never been in the plant or office, will not know what is out of place or what items aren't found in the area on a daily basis. Nor will he know where the hiding places are, or what areas the public has access to and therefore where the bomb is most likely to be placed. Also, few officers have actually received bomb search training, since this is not normally considered a patrol officer's function. The bomb squad also will not be familiar with the area, and you will lose valuable time waiting for them to arrive. If your search teams can identify a suspect device while the bomb squad is en route, then the experts can go to work as soon as they arrive.

There are many excellent publications on the training of bomb search teams. One of these is *Bomb Threats and Search Techniques,* published by the Bureau of Alcohol, Tobacco, and Firearms (BATF) and available from the U.S. Government Printing Office or your local BATF office listed under Federal Government in your telephone directory (Stock Number ATF P 7550.2 7/87). Another good source is U.S. Army Training Circular TC 19–5, *Bomb Threats,* published by the U.S. Army Military Police School at Fort McClellan, Alabama.

Most bomb threats are hoaxes, and when bombs are actually planted it is done by a disgruntled employee, an angry customer, or a sociopath. If a terrorist decides to target your assets for a bombing, there is seldom a warning before the bomb goes off. A terrorist will telephone you or the media *afterward* and take credit for the incident.

When responding to the scene of a bombing, your priorities include:

- Securing the area and preventing unauthorized entry.
- Evacuating and treating the injured.
- Searching immediately for possible secondary devices.
- Trying to prevent the destruction of evidence.

Obviously your immediate concern will be for the injured; since there may be secondary devices in the area you should try to move live victims to a safe place immediately. Individuals who die during the initial explosion should be left exactly as they are found. Your attention needs to be directed to the survivors. Also, the position of the dead bodies and their wounds may be important evidence during the criminal investigation.

Responsibility for tending the wounded should be assigned to a specific group of people, while your bomb search teams concentrate on combing the area for possible secondary devices. Secondary devices are detonated either with timers set to go off a short time after the primary explosion, or by remote control once the police are on the scene. Since most remote control devices must be located near the explosive device to be effective, you should also appoint several security personnel to surveil the immediate area and identify suspects or others persons who don't seem to belong. If you do spot a suspected terrorist, remember that this person is probably better armed than you are and that he or she may have a backup team in the area. Identify these people and try to contain and/or photograph them, but wait for the police to arrive before you attempt to apprehend them.

When a bomb explodes, a great deal of destruction can occur, and it may look as though the evidence has been destroyed by the bomb itself. This is not so. Bomb technicians and investigators can collect minute pieces of evidence that help them determine how the original bomb was built and detonated. Since most groups and bombers develop their personal style of building and using bombs, investigators may be able to identify the "signature" of the bomber during their investigation. To make sure these technicians have access to the evidence they need, treat the bombing as you would any other crime scene and secure the area immediately. No one should touch or move anything, including wires, springs, batteries, or other fragments; these may prove to be valuable clues.

KIDNAPPING AND HOSTAGE SITUATIONS

The immediate response to a hostage-taking situation is usually by the police or security officer who first arrives at the scene. This person should verify that this is a hostage situation, contain it, and notify his commander or dispatcher immediately. Management of the incident, as we have already discussed, will then revert to the emergency operations center, once it is activated, and you will prepare for the three phases of an incident response.

An organization that receives a claim that an executive or other person has been kidnapped or taken hostage should immediately notify the proper lead agency. If the incident occurs within the United States, that agency is the FBI. If it occurs outside of the U.S., you need to contact the U.S. Department of State.

The next two steps in your response should occur simultaneously. Attempt to verify that the person is actually missing and that he or she may be a hostage or kidnap victim. At the same time, move that person's family to an area safely away from the threat of additional abductions and from the calls by the media that will begin as soon as word of the incident is released. You also need to secure all sensitive facilities and other high-risk personnel in the geographic area where the incident occurred. A private sector organization will then work with the FBI to resolve a situation that occurs within the U.S., or with the U.S. Department of State and possibly the host country if the incident occurs outside of the U.S. A private organization should always go through the appropriate lead agency when confronted with a kidnapping or hostage-taking. Never work directly with the host country unless the Department of State is involved or with outside security consultants who tell you not to include these agencies in your response.

If ransom is demanded, you may be confronted with a unique problem. In many countries it is illegal to pay ransom to terrorists, and if you do pay, the company's assets in that country can be nationalized. Knowing this, terrorists will occasionally suggest that the ransom be paid in a third country. For example, if a kidnapping occurs in a Latin American country where paying ransom to terrorists is illegal, they may suggest that you deposit the money in a bank account in Europe. The victim will then be released in the country where the incident occurred. Still, if that government learns you have paid the ransom, they may nationalize all of your assets or place charges against your executives for violation of their criminal statutes.

Another consideration in making a ransom payment is that you must make sure the person who makes the decision has the authority to do so. There have been several situations where stockholder suits have been initiated against corporate executives, stating that the executive was not empowered to make decisions regarding the payment of ransom. Since numerous legal questions must be answered before a ransom can be paid, you will need the advice of your attorneys and the representatives of the appropriate lead agency. However, the ultimate decision on whether or not a ransom is paid will probably rest with the corporate executives.[4]

Hostage-taking situations are usually resolved, one way or the other, within a matter of days. We know where the terrorists and the hostages are and the tactical options available. If the matter is not resolved through negotiation, or if the terrorists start killing hostages, then the tactical force option is used. However, kidnapping situations such as those we witnessed in Latin America during the 1970s and in Lebanon in the past decade can last for months or even years. The organization should be prepared to support and protect the victims' families for as long as the incident lasts, and to provide counseling and the other support services that may be needed afterward to assist the victims in returning from captivity and to minimize the post-trauma shock syndrome that may result from the experience.

TERRORIST ATTACKS

Most terrorist attacks are of a short duration since they rely on hit-and-run tactics. A tactical cell doesn't have enough people to overwhelm a substantial police or security force, but man-for-man they will usually have them outgunned. Police and security personnel armed with revolvers or automatic pistols find themselves facing terrorists with submachine guns and grenades.

In some cases, as with the Japanese Red Army attack at Lod Airport in Israel, the synagogue attack in Istanbul in 1986, and the Abu Nidal attacks on the Rome and Vienna airports, the terrorists are not expected to escape. The leaders are willing to sacrifice the tactical cell by letting them be captured or, preferably, having them die as martyrs during the attack.

In other cases the group does intend to escape after the attack, and elaborate escape plans will have been rehearsed before the incident. This was the case in the series of Black Liberation Army ambushes of police officers in the United States during the 1970s, and in Action Direct attacks on INTERPOL headquarters in May 1986. Part of your counterterrorism plan should be to identify and secure all escape routes if an attack occurs against one of your assets. A private organization should coordinate these plans with the appropriate law enforcement agencies in your areas of operation.

Remember, too, that many terrorist attacks are used as a diversion in an attempt to draw law enforcement and security personnel away from the primary target. Train all of your security and law enforcement people to secure their immediate area of responsibility, and make sure you have special plans to secure sensitive areas and high-risk personnel whenever an incident takes place.

PUTTING IT ALL TOGETHER

When a crisis occurs it brings out either the best or the worst in the people who must respond to and manage it. This is especially true during a terrorist incident because of the numerous political implications and the media impact of the event. Your CMT members and all other personnel responsible for dealing with these situations must be carefully selected and trained so that they are prepared to perform at their best when called upon to function in these roles during an actual incident. If the threat management committee has been allowed to do its job during the anti-terrorism phase, your response during counterterrorism operations will be greatly enhanced.

IMPLEMENTATION CHECKLIST

1. Consider how you would respond at each phase of the counterterrorism response.
   a. Initial phase.
   b. Transfer of jurisdiction.
   c. Committing additional assets.
2. Personnel prepared to respond to the incident should include:
   a. Tactical teams.
   b. Crisis management team.
   c. Support personnel.
   d. Reserve forces.
3. Prepare your plans to respond to:
   a. Bombings and bomb threats.
   b. Kidnapping and hostage situations.
   c. Terrorist attacks.
4. To put it all together:
   a. Make sure your CMT and EOC are ready to function.
   b. Validate your plans and operations on a regular basis.

EPILOGUE

As the characters in our fictional scenario attempt to recover from the shock of Friday morning's events, let us take a hard look at just what happened in Pleasantville. First of all, how realistic are the events that have been described?

Are the terrorist groups in the real world as heavily armed as the Aryan Peoples Party? You can bet on it! The Black Liberation Army used M-3 Grease Guns to kill police officers in the early 1970s. More recently, members of groups such as the Brotherhood of Silence and the Covenant, Sword, and the Arm of the Lord were known to be armed with multiple automatic weapons, hand grenades, and other weapons ranging from rocket launchers to crossbows. In almost all cases, when a police officer is in a shoot-out with a terrorist, the terrorist has the weapons advantage.

Would such events really take place in a small town in mid-America rather than in New York, San Francisco, or another major city? In reality, terrorism is not limited to major urban centers. Posse Comitatus compounds dot the landscape in rural mid-America today. And twenty years ago the Republic of New Africa, a black militant organization, found its home not in the ghettos of New York but in the rural towns of Mississippi, in the same areas where the Ku Klux Klan operates. No community is immune from becoming the home or the target of a terrorist group.

Now let us evaluate the work of the threat management committee: What did they do right? What went wrong? How could they have been better prepared to deal with Friday's events?

Pleasantville authorities did recognize the need for a community-wide threat management committee and were well on their way to establishing an effective response to the threat. But they waited too long before establishing the committee and the individuals involved were hampered by the political realities of threat management and emergency operations. The number one priority on the mayor's agenda was to get reelected; he didn't want his constituency alarmed about a bunch of right-wing radicals. Toten Industries cut back the security budget just when their security manager was trying to increase the effectiveness of his department.

In the real world, the amount of money and support available to the antiterrorism planner is too often based on a knee-jerk response; that is, it is directly related to the last incident. If the incident was recent, the support will be there. If it's been some time since the last incident, or if an incident has never occurred, then support may be lacking. One way to circumvent this problem is to build antiterrorism planning into a crime prevention program, since most managers in the public and the private sector recognize the need for crime prevention. If you incorporate anti-terrorism programs into crime prevention programs, you will find less resistance and will usually end up with a better all-around program.

Another political reality was the "turf battles" that took place among TMC members. The FBI thought they should run the show, while the Pleasantville Police Department believed they should be in charge, since it was their town. Turf battles do occur, but on this and other committees, professionalism usually prevails and the job gets done.

The foundation of an effective antiterrorism program is good intelligence; you must know as much as possible about your adversary. But, as the key players in our scenario learned, that's not an easy task. All federal agencies have regulations that restrict the information they can collect and maintain, and guidelines as to how and when that information can be shared with others. These restrictions are necessary if we are to maintain the ideals on which our society was founded. If we are also going to protect that society, however, then a balance between the rights of individuals and the need for the collection of criminal intelligence must be achieved.

The collection of intelligence on the Aryan Peoples Party by the FBI was obviously justified. The APP had already committed crimes, including bombings and bank robberies, and it was dealing with foreign governments and terrorist groups whose interests were contrary to the American government. But even when the collection of intelligence is justified, the dissemination of that information may not be. The FBI had sufficient information to conduct an investigation of the APP, but since the investigation was still in progress, they were restricted from sharing that information with other agencies.

Collection of intelligence on the Citizens Against Chemical Warfare organization could not be done. The automatic collection of intelligence on special-interest groups is not acceptable in our society, even if those groups have goals and objectives contrary to U.S. policy—*unless* they are suspected of being involved in criminal activity. If the CACW's connections to the Cuban Intelligence Service (DGI) had been suspected, intelligence collection would have been justified, and the committee would have had more data available.

Jack Pardue, on the other hand, did manage to collect extensive intelligence on the Pleasantville threat management committee. Rest assured that in the real world terrorist groups do the same. They are experts at using all of the intelligence collection methods we have discussed, and they are not restricted by the ethical, moral, or legal constraints that impact on law enforcement agencies.

If intelligence is the foundation of an antiterrorism program, then operations security is its cornerstone. The committee was fortunate to have Lieutenant Colonel Marsh's assistance in developing an OPSEC program. Unfortunately, the committee waited too long to do this and Pardue already had the information he needed to plan his attacks. This became a major chink in their armor. (Note that Pardue fully understood OPSEC and had initiated OPSEC programs for the Aryan Peoples Party.)

The TMC also waited too long to activate the emergency operations center. The original plan should have called for activation of the EOC several days before the incident was expected. And when the FBI's informant disappeared, activation of the center and tightening of security at all potential targets should have been considered. Remember our model for developing a terrorism counteraction mind-set: Once you think you have the adversary figured out, expect the unexpected!

In keeping with the concept of expecting the unexpected, the committee should have been prepared for multiple events. Terrorist groups use diversionary tactics and will often go to extremes to confuse and frustrate the authorities. Simultaneous attacks and bombs being detonated at different locations are methods used to accomplish that objective.

The building where the EOC was located was not adequately protected. The entire building should have been secured, not just the floor on which the center was located. The APP was able to plant bombs in the building and wreak additional havoc on the operation of the emergency response.

In addition, the committee did not plan effectively for the handling of the media. This was never mentioned during their planning sessions. When a real incident occurs, the media will always arrive right after the bombs go off. A public information or public affairs officer plays an important role in planning for this contingency and should be included on the threat management committee and in the emergency operations center.

A major problem experienced by the members of the threat management committee was overcoming their own ethnocentric limitations. To understand the problem of terrorism and to combat it, you must learn to think like your terrorist adversary. You must try to understand their fanatical obsession with their cause and the lack of moral and ethical restraints demonstrated by most group members. Blowing airplanes out of the sky gets people's attention. Murdering children in a nursery gets the front page of the newspaper. Always remember that media attention is a primary terrorist goal.

On the positive side, the committee did perform a number of important tasks in a short period of time. They developed a threat statement, developed systems to conduct vulnerability surveys, worked on potential scenarios, and prepared for the crisis management response. The initial committee also recognized the need to bring additional agencies into the picture. (Unfortunately, they left out the sheriff's department; if it had been included, the sheriff's death might have been averted.)

At all times, the committee was cognizant of the need to insure that they were operating in a legal manner. They were careful not to violate the rights of groups or individuals. An overzealous committee may get the job done but in the process it may substantiate the often-made claim by terrorists that the system is oppressive. By violating the rights of others, future opportunities to prosecute terrorists and their supporters may be jeopardized.

Let us hope that the Pleasantville threat management committee also included damage control measures in their contingency plans so the community can get back to normal in the shortest possible time. In spite of the anger and embarrassment they may feel at this time, it is important to prepare an extensive after-action analysis of their activities prior to the infamous Friday and their responses to those events. This analysis can then be shared with other law enforcement agencies and antiterrorism planners so they all can learn from the experience.

Somewhere in the real world, a Jack Pardue and others like him exist. These individuals are totally dedicated to their beliefs, and they are committed to the concept of targeted actions, or what we call terrorism, to accomplish their mission. Some of them are supremacists, of various races; some are separatists; some even have a legitimate cause. But they are all terrorists and, as a result, the enemies of the free world.

Jack Pardue lives on to initiate Armageddon somewhere else. The Citizens Against Chemical Warfare are grouping for demonstrations and confrontations in another town. And Pleasantville is licking its wounds and trying to return to normal.

The events have been fictitious. Let's hope they remain that way.

APPENDIX A

TERRORIST GROUPS

This appendix will provide information on certain organizations and terrorist groups referred to in the text. It is not meant to be a comprehensive listing of the groups that are active in the world. In fact, many of the groups listed are no longer active but have been included for historical reference. For a list of groups that currently present a threat to U.S. assets, the reader should obtain the most recent copies of *Patterns of Global Terrorism* from the U.S. Department of State and *Terrorism in the United States* from the Federal Bureau of Investigation.

NATIONALIST AND SEPARATIST GROUPS

Euskadi Ta Askatasuna (ETA)

The "Basque Homeland and Freedom" group, ETA, is an insurgent terrorist group that has been active in Spanish terrorism since the 1960s, although the roots of the group date back several centuries. The actual Basque region includes the northwest corner of Spain and three provinces in France. The Basques have a separate language and culture, which have been suppressed repeatedly under Spanish rule and most recently under General Franco. The ETA was formed in 1962, inspired by Castro's success in Cuba. Members operate in three-person cells and their objective is to create a free Basque territory through the use of terrorism and other forms of violence. Basques have been trained in PLO camps and are known to have links with the Red Resistance Front in Holland and with the IRA and Action Direct.

Irish National Liberation Army (INLA)

The INLA is the military wing of the Irish Republican Socialist Party. It was formed in 1975 and is committed to creating a socialist state in all of Ireland by pushing the British out of Ulster and overthrowing the government of the Republic of Ireland. The group subscribes to violence as a means of achieving those objectives.

Irish Republican Army (IRA)/Provisional IRA (PIRA)

The primary objective of the IRA and the PIRA is to force the British out of Ulster (the northern six counties of Ireland) and unify all the counties into the Republic of Ireland. Whereas the IRA operates in Ulster (their headquarters are in Dublin), the "Provos" believe the objective can be accomplished only by taking the battle to the U.K. Most of the Irish terrorist attacks in England and Europe in recent years have been the work of the PIRA. The IRA/PIRA receives assistance from active and passive supporters in the U.S. Irish-American community. Group members have been involved in weapons robberies, gun running, and narcotics trafficking in or through the U.S.

Sikhs

Sikhism is a Hindu sect that was founded in northern India, the Punjab region, around A.D. 1500. Sikhism is based on belief in one God and a rejection of the caste system and idolatry. As terrorists, Sikhs are one of the most active groups in the world today. They have been responsible for more than a thousand deaths in the past few years while operating throughout India (although primarily in the Punjab) and in Great Britain, the United States, and Canada. They place bombs on airliners (one bombing resulted in 329 deaths); assassinate Indian politicians, diplomats, police, and military personnel; incite riots and demonstrations; and are well trained, well armed, and highly committed. Their objective is to establish a separate Sikh nation in the Punjab.

Tamils

The Tamils, an ethnic group in Sri Lanka (formerly Ceylon) and southern India, are currently "at war" with the Sri Lankan government. The active support group for the movement, the People's Liberation Organization of Tamil Eelam, is a Marxist-Leninist organization that opposes the free enterprise system and the Sri Lanka membership in the British Commonwealth. The military arm of the organization, the Liberation Tigers of Tamil Eelam, is committed to creating a separate Tamil state through terrorism and guerrilla warfare. The Tamils have operated primarily in Sri Lanka; however, they train in and may receive support from India.

EUROPEAN LEFT-WING GROUPS

Action Direct (AD)

Action Direct (AD) was organized in France in 1979 by Jean-Marc Rouillan, a former member of the International Revolutionary Action Group. The credo of the group is to "wreck society through *direct action* by destroying its institutions and the men who serve it." It is a key group in the European terror alliance and is a left-wing anarchist force. It maintains contacts with the Communist Combatant Cells (CCC), RAF, BR, ETA, and several Middle Eastern groups, including the Lebanese Armed Revolutionary Faction (FARL). Members engage in bombings, assassinations, and sabotage against military, political, diplomatic, and industrial targets. There are twenty-five to fifty hard-core members and a substantial active and passive support structure. They have assassinated U.S. personnel, and most recently a French general and a major industrialist. Most of the group's leaders are currently serving long prison sentences in France.

Brigate Rosse (BR)

During the 1970s and early 1980s, the Brigate Rosse was Italy's largest left-wing terrorist group. It was organized in the 1960s under the leadership of Renato Curcio as a hard-core spin-off of the Italian Communist party. The group adapted the Tupamaros organizational structure of columns rather than cells and had major columns of 100 to 250 members each in most major Italian cities. The group has connections with most left-wing European terrorists, with the PFLP, and with the Eastern bloc. It has received state support from Libya and Bulgaria and is suspected of carrying out operations under the direction of the Bulgarian Secret Police. This is the group that was responsible for the kidnapping and murder of Aldo Moro and the kidnapping of Brig. Gen. James Dozier. Although the BR has operated only in Italy, group members have served in the Sandinista Army in Nicaragua. As a result of police crackdowns in recent years, many of the leaders are now in prison and the operational capabilities of the group have diminished.

Communist Combatant Cells (CCC)

In 1984 Pierre Carette, a Belgian national, asked his AD friend Jean-Marc Rouillan to let AD operate against targets in Belgium. Instead, Rouillan suggested that Carette form a new group, and the CCC was born. The group consisted of fewer than twenty-five hard-core members but was responsible for a number of bombings and acts of sabotage until Carette was captured in December 1985. This is a leftist group with ties, through AD, to other European groups. Most of its attacks have been low-risk operations against soft targets, and much of its funding came from a series of bank robberies. It claims that most of its intelligence comes from open-source information, and, unlike other terrorist groups in Europe today, most of its bombs have been detonated at times and places designed to minimize the risk of casualties. As new leadership emerges, the group may once again become active.

Red Army Faction (RAF)

Originally the Baader-Meinhof gang, this is one of the premier terrorist groups in the world. The hard-core membership is estimated to be about twenty-five people, and they have direct links to other European groups (including the Communist Combatant Cells in Belgium, Brigate Rosse in Italy, and Action Direct in France) and with Palestinian groups, including the PFLP. They have received state support from the Soviet bloc and from Libya. This is a Marxist-Leninist group dedicated to the armed anti-imperialist revolution. Members are involved in bombings, assassinations, kidnappings, and sabotage, and in recent years they have increased their tendency to place and time devices to maximize casualties. The RAF targets NATO, the U.S., West Germany, and any other victims that suit its objectives at any particular time.

Revolutionary Cells (RZ)

The Revolutionary Cells (RZ) is a small group operating in the Federal Republic of Germany. Members work in cells of two to five people each, and there may be as many as twenty cells currently underground. Many members are suspected of being part-time terrorists. The group has a leftist orientation and believes that revolution will best be achieved through the actions of a small group. Members are also anti-Zionist and have attacked Jewish targets. They manufacture small bombs, which is their preferred tactic, and have hit military, political, and business targets. The group is suspected of having connections with the IRA.

EUROPEAN RIGHT-WING GROUPS

The Charles Martel Club
This French right-wing group was named for the medieval warrior-hero who halted the Muslim advance from Spain in the period A.D. 732 to 739. Some of the members were former soldiers in the French-Algerian war. The group has incited brawls and student riots in Paris and was responsible for at least one bombing at the Air Algeria office in Marseilles.

FANE/FNE
This is another French right-wing organization. It primarily opposes Jewish interests in France and has been responsible for a number of attacks on Jewish institutions, including the machine-gun attacks on at least five buildings in Paris and the bombing of a synagogue. The group has also engaged in vandalism against Jewish targets and may have taken credit for several incidents actually perpetrated by Arab terrorists.

Hoffman Military-Sports Group
This West German group was named for its founder and leader, Karl Heinz Hoffman; its most infamous act was the Octoberfest bombing on 26 September 1979 that resulted in 13 deaths and more than 300 injuries when a bomb exploded in a Munich beer hall. The bombing led to the arrest of Hoffman and ten other members. This group has maintained contacts with groups within the PLO and has relied on the PLO for training and other support. In fact, at one point members of the Hoffman Group and the Red Army Faction were training in PLO camps in Lebanon at the same time. One of the sources of funding for the Hoffman Group was the sale of used trucks to al-Fatah. The group has engaged in bombings, assassinations, and destruction of Jewish interests (including defacing cemetery markers). One member was also arrested for the firebombing of a Vietnamese refugee hotel, which resulted in the deaths of several children. A leader of the Hoffman Group is known to have attended a seminar at the Aryan Nations compound in the U.S. and is suspected of having ties with the right-wing movement in Canada.

Ordine Nuovo (New Order)

One of the most significant right-wing groups in Italy is Ordine Nuovo, a group that used to call itself Ordine Nero (Black Order). The group received weapons, money, and training from Libya (which was also supporting the Brigate Rosse at the time), and members may have been involved in the Bologna train station bombing on 1 August 1979 in which 76 people were killed and 188 injured. An investigation of that bombing by Italian police showed that it may have been planned by a French member of FANE (who was also a senior police official) and carried out by French, West German, and Italian right-wing terrorists. The Bologna bombing investigation indicates that there is an operational linkage among right-wing groups in that part of the world, and that the coalition has direct ties to Libyan and Palestinian terrorists.

PALESTINIAN GROUPS

Abu Nidal Group

One of the bloodiest Palestinian groups is the Abu Nidal Group, headed by Sabri al-Banna. Al-Banna adapted the name Abu Nidal, which means the father of the struggle. The group is currently sponsored by Syria (its former sponsor was Libya). Some of its operations are carried out in support of the Syrian intelligence organization. This group is anti-Arafat, and Abu Nidal has issued a warrant for Arafat's assassination. Arafat has also issued a warrant for the assassination of Nidal. The group has assassinated moderate PLO leaders, and Nidal even had his brother-in-law killed when he defected from the group. Abu Nidal was responsible for the airport massacres in Rome and Vienna in December 1985 and for the attempted bombing of an El Al jet at Heathrow Airport in 1986. The group has several hundred hard-core members and has been responsible for at least twenty-five major terrorist incidents since 1976. The most horrifying attack was the bombing of a Gulf Air Boeing 737 on 23 September 1983, in which 111 people were killed. It is estimated that Syria provides almost $12 million per year to support the Abu Nidal Group.

Lebanese Armed Revolutionary Faction (FARL)

This group was formed by George Ibrahim Abdullah, who is currently in prison in France. The group, which receives support from Syria, is connected with Action Direct and was responsible for the ten bombings in Paris in September 1986 that resulted in 10 deaths and 257 wounded. Abdullah is currently serving a four-year sentence for possession of false identity papers and for associating with criminals.

Palestinian Liberation Front (PLF)
This group is aligned with the PLO and its leader is Abu el-Abbas. It is headquartered in Iraq but also maintains commands in Tunisia and South Yemen. This group was responsible for the attack on the *Achille Lauro* and has threatened to bring terrorism to the U.S. Total membership is about 200 hard-core fighters.

Palestinian Liberation Organization (PLO)
The PLO is actually a coalition of numerous Palestinian groups aligned with Yassir Arafat's leadership. Al-Fatah is the group directly under the leadership of Arafat; it is a Soviet-supported terrorist organization that receives additional support from Arab nations and Palestinians around the world. The PLO has also received support from the People's Republic of China in the form of arms, ammunition, and money. Splinter groups of the PLO operate throughout the world, but their primary target is Israeli and Jewish interests.

Popular Front for the Liberation of Palestine (PFLP)
The PFLP was organized by George Habash, a physician trained at the American University in Beirut. Habash was the first leader to export Palestinian terrorism when in 1968 he sent a unit to hijack an El Al airplane in Rome. Since then, the PFLP has engaged in acts throughout Europe and the Middle East. The group established connections with left-wing groups in Europe at the end of the 1960s and has trained both left- and right-wing terrorists from around the world.

Popular Front for the Liberation of Palestine—General Command
Ahmad Jibril formed this group in 1968 when he became disenchanted with Habash's leadership in the PFLP. The group numbers about 500 and its political objective is the destruction of Israel. Members have been responsible for a number of terrorist actions ranging from the use of letter bombs to the bomb that destroyed Pan American Flight 103 in December 1988.

ISLAMIC GROUPS

Hezbollah

Hezbollah, or the Party of God, is an Iranian-directed group that operates in Lebanon. It receives support and direction from the Iranian government and has attacked U.S. and other Western targets along with Israeli interests in the region. Hezbollah may be expanded to operate in other parts of the world after the Iran-Iraq war ends.

Islamic Jihad

The Jihad is actually a coalition of groups supported by Iran. At least eight groups are included in the coalition, including the following: Movement of Hezbollah, based south of Beirut; Islamic Amal, the Islamic Army, located in Baalbek; Jundallah, Soldiers of God; Kawar Alnasr, Forces of Victory; Revolutionary Arab Brigades, located in southern Lebanon; Ansar al Iman, Supporters of the Iman; and Hezboaldawa, Party of the Called.

LATIN AMERICAN GROUPS

April 19th Movement (M-19)

This Colombian Marxist-Leninist group (M-19) is supported by both the Soviet Union and Cuba. Its founder, Jamie Bateman, was trained in Moscow. Two of the more spectacular events by the group include the lengthy takeover of the Dominican Republic Embassy in Bogota in 1980 and the assault on the Justice Palace in 1985. The assault on the Justice Palace was conducted under contract to the Drug Mafia in Colombia; the group was paid $5 million for the action. The M-19 has become deeply involved with drug trafficking in the Western Hemisphere; members themselves traffic in narcotics and provide protection for the Drug Mafia in Colombia.

Frente Farabundo Marti De Liberacion Nacional (FMLN)

This Salvadoran group is a Marxist-Leninist organization supported by Cuba, Nicaragua, and the Soviet bloc. The group operates primarily in El Salvador but has attacked the U.S. Embassy in Costa Rica.

Sendero Luminoso

Sendero Luminoso (Shining Path) is a radical Maoist organization that claims total independence from state support but, in fact, has received weapons and other logistical support from the Eastern bloc. The group was founded by a university professor, Abimael Guzman, who now goes by the name Gonzalo. The group went underground in 1977 when it lost control of Huamanga University, where Guzman was a professor, to a rival Marxist group. Since that time it has grown into a large guerrilla organization and has been responsible for at least 10,000 deaths. The group is deeply involved in drug trafficking and provides protection— for a price—to drug trafficking mafias in Peru.

Tupamaros

The Tupamaros of Uruguay was one of the leading terrorist groups in the late 1960s and early 1970s. Numbering about 3,000 people, the group terrorized the nation into a military dictatorship in 1972, its members claiming their role to be that of freedom fighters. The group provided the model for the organization of other groups such as the Brigate Rosse in Italy.

PUERTO RICAN GROUPS

Armed Forces of National Liberation (FALN)

The FALN is the primary Puerto Rican terrorist group operating in the U.S. It introduced itself in New York City on 16 October 1974 with the bombing of five banks. Its bombings in the U.S. have caused considerable damage and at least four deaths and fifty-seven injuries. Although the leaders of the group are now in prison, the cadre developed a plan in June 1986 to break the leaders out of the prison at Fort Leavenworth using an elaborate plot involving three helicopters. Two of the helicopters were to serve as gunships while the third extracted the leaders from the prison yard. Although the plot was detected, most of the group members involved are still at large. The group has received direct support from Cuba since its inception.

Ejercito Popular Boricua—Macheteros

This group is the most violent terrorist organization on the island of Puerto Rico. It has conducted bombings, sabotage, rocket attacks, and armed robberies. It has destroyed nine Air National Guard jets at the ANG Base at the Muniz Airport, Puerto Rico, and robbed an armored car in West Hartford, Connecticut, of approximately $7 million. The group is supported by Cuba, and when the cadre involved in the West Hartford robbery was arrested in the U.S., Puerto Rico, and Mexico, the leader of the group emerged in Havana, where he held a press conference. This group has bombed U.S. targets in Puerto Rico and in the U.S. and participated in the shooting of a U.S. Army major in San Juan in 1985.

National Liberation Movement (MLN)

The MLN is a separatist group that advocates the use of violence to achieve the independence of Puerto Rico. It actively supports terrorist groups on the island and the FALN in the United States.

Organization of Volunteers for the Puerto Rican Revolution (OVRP)

This Puerto Rico–based group is affiliated with the Macheteros and participated in the attack on the U.S. Army major in 1985. The group primarily uses bombs against military recruiting stations; however, it was also responsible for the ambush of a group of U.S. Navy personnel at Sebana Seca on 2 December 1979, an action conducted with the Macheteros.

RIGHT-WING GROUPS IN THE UNITED STATES

Aryan Nation (AN)

Also known as the Church of Jesus Christ Christian, the AN was founded in the mid-1970s by Richard Butler. The church and group are aligned with the Identity Movement, and they have links with almost all other ultraright groups in the U.S. and Canada, and with the Hoffman Sports Group in the FRG. The group is dedicated to forming a whites-only Nation in the northwestern United States and has reportedly met with the nation of Islam to divide up the country. The AN conducts a prison ministry, seeking to recruit members of the Aryan Brotherhood, a white supremacy group that operates within many prison systems in the U.S. The AN holds an annual summer convention at its Hayden Lake, Idaho, compound, inviting ultraright and neo-Nazi groups from across the U.S. to participate. It was at the 1983 meeting that the Order emerged.

Christian Identity Movement
This loose affiliation of "churches" and small groups of right-wing extremists has its basis in the nineteenth-century doctrine of British Israelism. Group members believe that the Aryan race is the lost tribe of Israel and that God has provided a specific destiny for them—to have a separate homeland where they will maintain racial purity. Most other races are referred to as the "mud races." Members also believe that there is a Zionist conspiracy to control the world.

Christian Patriots Defense League
This group was founded in 1977 by "Johnny Bob" Harrell and is headquartered at his farm in Flora, Illinois. The group is an extremist survival group involved in paramilitary training, and it claims to be preparing for the collapse of the American system. The collapse will be caused by a Communist-Zionist conspiracy and will culminate in a racial war for which white Americans should be preparing. The organization has opened additional "bases" in Missouri, about twenty-five miles from Fort Leonard Wood, and in West Virginia.

The Covenant, the Sword, and the Arm of the Lord
This group was founded by Jim Ellison in 1975 as a religious group associated with the Identity Church Movement. Members have interacted with other extremist groups, including the KKK, Aryan Nation, Posse Comitatus, and the Brotherhood. They provided automatic weapons and other supplies to many of these groups while operating from a 224-acre compound in Arkansas. The compound is said to have contained mine fields, machine-gun bunkers, and armored cars. When federal agents searched the compound (after being delayed while securing a search warrant), much of this evidence had apparently been hidden or removed. The compound was sold in 1986 and the group has disbanded.

Ku Klux Klan (KKK)
The KKK is the oldest terrorist group in the United States. It is no longer one unified Klan but actually consists of three major Klan groups and a number of small splinter groups. The KKK serves as a breeding ground for other right-wing groups, and most leaders of other groups currently active in the U.S. have a Klan background. In many cases they continue to have dual memberships in the KKK and the other group to which they

belong. Total membership in the various Klan factions is estimated to be 8,000 to 10,000.

The Order (the Brotherhood, the Brotherhood of Silence)

The founder of the Brotherhood, Robert J. Mathews, took the name of the organization from the *Turner Diaries,* a book published by the National Alliance. He also adapted the tactics used in the book and had members formally sign a declaration of war against ZOG. The group was responsible for a series of bank and armored-car robberies, the murder of several people, counterfeiting, and several bombings. Although most of the members, including the leadership, are either dead or in jail, a member of the group robbed a bank in July 1986 to continue to support the Order's activities. Robert Mathews died in a shoot-out with federal authorities on an island in Puget Sound on 7 December 1984.

Order of the Rising Star

This small neo-Nazi group in the Chicago area was active for a brief period during the early 1970s.

Posse Comitatus (Sheriff's Posse Comitatus)

This group was started in Seattle in 1968 by Henry Lamont "Mike" Beach, who sold charters for $21 and Posse badges for $6.50. Posse members oppose federal taxation and recognize the county sheriff as the highest office of law enforcement under the Constitution. One member, Gordon Kahl, was responsible for several shoot-outs with law enforcement authorities during which three law enforcement officials were killed. Kahl himself died when he was surrounded by agents in a farmhouse in Smithville, Arkansas. In May 1986, a Posse husband and wife team took an entire elementary school hostage in Cokeville, Wyoming. Both died during the incident. Most group members are armed vigilantes and survivalists; some of them live on Posse compounds waiting for the "big war."

White Patriots Party (WPP)

The WPP was founded in the early 1980s by Glen Miller of Angier, North Carolina, and may have had up to 250 members. The objective of the group was to form a separate white nation. In 1985, Miller was convicted on state charges and ordered not to associate with any white supremacist organizations. In January 1987, five members of the group were indicted on federal charges of conspiring to obtain stolen U.S.

military weapons and equipment. Miller is currently in prison and the group is no longer a force in the right-wing community.

LEFT-WING GROUPS IN THE UNITED STATES

Armed Resistance Unit (ARU)
This group emerged on 26 April 1983, when it claimed responsibility for a bombing at Fort McNair in Washington, D.C. It is a leftist group that opposes U.S. involvement in Latin America. The group participated in a joint action on 17 August 1983, when, with the FMLN (at least they claim to have been operating with the FMLN), it planted a bomb at the Navy Yard in Washington, D.C. They were also responsible for an ARU/FMLN bombing at the nation's Capitol that caused extensive damage on 7 November 1983. The group is probably composed of part-time terrorists with ideological ties to Cuba.

Black Liberation Army (BLA)
This group has been inactive for the past several years but continues to maintain a safe-house network in the eastern U.S. The leader of the group, Joanne Chesimard, escaped from prison in New Jersey, where she had murdered a highway patrol officer. Unlike other terrorist groups, the BLA does not engage in bombing. Its preferred tactic is to ambush police officers. The group has received support from Cuba and participates in the M19CO.

Black Panthers
Founded in 1966 by Huey Newton and Bobby Seale in Oakland, California, the group quickly had chapters across the United States. Members have been convicted of bombings, murders, and other terrorist actions. The group lost much of its power as a result of factional infighting during the 1970s.

May 19th Communist Organization (M19CO)
The M19CO was formed as a coalition of members from the Weather Underground Organization, Black Liberation Army, Republic of New Africa, and Black Panthers. The group, which is supported by Cuba and has connections with the FALN, also goes by the name Revolutionary Armed Task Force, which it adapted while trying to form a coalition with other groups including the Brigate Rosse, Red Army Faction, and PFLP.

The M19CO was responsible for the 1981 Brinks' robbery at Nyack, New York, in which three people were murdered.

Nation of Islam (NI)
The leader of this black militant organization is Louis Farrakhan, who maintains close ties with Muammar Qaddafi. Reportedly, Libya gave NI a gift of at least $6 million in 1984 when Qaddafi was the featured speaker, via satellite, at the annual NI meeting in Chicago. During that speech, Qaddafi called for all black soldiers in U.S. uniforms to rise up against their imperialist suppressors. Farrakhan declared during a speech in Washington, D.C., on 22 July 1985 that he would chop off the head of any black leader who opposed him. Farrakhan has also established ties with Syria.

Republic of New Africa (RNA)
Founded in 1968, the RNA was a black separatist group. Following a police raid on their headquarters in August 1970, eleven members of the group were charged with murder, assault, and waging war against the State of Mississippi. The group is no longer in operation.

Revolutionary Armed Task Force (RATF)
This group, formed by members of the WUO, Black Panthers, RNA, and the BLA after the WUO inversion, considered itself the military arm of the May 19th Communist Organization. Although the group's existence was short-lived, they were responsible for the robbery of a Brinks armored car on October 20, 1981, at Nyack, New York, during which three people were killed. Most of the RATF members were captured within days after the robbery. One member, Samuel Smith, died in a shoot-out with police in Queens, New York, just two days after the Brinks incident.

Symbionese Liberation Army (SLA)
This group's most famous action was the kidnapping of Patricia Hearst. It was a left-wing group originally founded to promote prison reform but it quickly turned to criminal activities. Most of the members are either dead or have served or are serving prison sentences.

Weather Underground Organization (WUO)
Originally named the Weathermen by its first leader, Mark Rudd, the group's name was changed by its second leader, Bernadine Dohrn, who thought the previous name was sexist. The group was responsible for the

"Days of Rage" at the Democratic National Convention in Chicago from October 8 to 11, 1969. The Weather Underground was one of the most active groups in the U.S. during the 1970s and responsible for a number of bombings. In 1976 the group began experiencing a series of internal disagreements that resulted in its "inversion" in 1979—part of the group remained underground to continue functioning as a clandestine organization while other members, including Dohrn, surrendered to authorities. Most of those who surrendered were given minimum sentences (Dohrn was given three years' probation and a fine); most of those who remained underground became members of the May 19th Communist Movement and its military arm, the Revolutionary Armed Task Force.

OTHER GROUPS IN THE UNITED STATES

Jewish Defense League (JDL)
Since its founding by Meir Kahane in 1968, the JDL has been an organized extremist group operating within the U.S., with an organizational structure that crosses the entire country. The motto of the group is "Never Again." Primary targets have been Soviet and Arab interests, but members have also attacked former Nazis and other ultraright targets. The group engages in assassinations, bombings, and vandalism. The JDL now conducts paramilitary training in California and in the Catskill Mountains on a regular basis and is forming a hard-core cadre of trained members. Of the seven terrorist incidents investigated by the FBI in 1985, four of the five bombings were attributed to the JDL or its splinter groups. These incidents, which took place in California, New Jersey, and New York, resulted in two deaths and nine injuries. The totals for *all* terrorist incidents investigated by the FBI in 1985 were two deaths and ten injuries (the other injury resulted from a rocket attack by OVRP in Puerto Rico). Splinter groups operate under names such as the Jewish Armed Resistance, Jewish Direct Action, and the Jewish Executioners With Silence.

United Freedom Front (UFF)
The targets of the UFF were corporate offices and military reserve and recruiting facilities. The group claimed a number of left-wing causes, including protest against the apartheid policies of South Africa and against U.S. imperialism and militarism. It was responsible for a series of bombings and bank robberies from 1975 through 1984, and for the murders

of at least two police officers. Members of the group are currently in prison.

OTHER INTERNATIONAL GROUPS

Armenian Secret Army for the Liberation of Armenia (ASALA)

The ASALA was formed in 1975 in Beirut and has strong ties with the PFLP. It has attacked Turkish targets around the world in retaliation for the massacre of a large number of Armenians by Turkish soldiers in 1896 and again in 1915. The group has been responsible for assassinations and bombings in the United States.

Croation Freedom Fighters (CFF)

The CFF is devoted to the reestablishment of a state of Croatia in what is now an area within Yugoslavia. Fifteen members of the group were arrested in 1982, and the group has not been responsible for attacks in the U.S. since that time.

Japanese Red Army (JRA)

This group was formed in 1971 by Fasako Shigenobu. It has been sponsored by the Popular Front for the Liberation of Palestine, North Korea, and Libya. The group has been responsible for a number of terrorist attacks, including the Lod Airport massacre in May 1972, the bomb planted in April 1988 at the U.S. servicemen's club in Naples that killed five people, and the July 1988 rocket attack against the U.S. Embassy in Madrid. Ya Kikumura, a JRA member, was arrested in New Jersey in 1988 while reportedly en route to plant bombs in the New York City area.

Justice Commandos of the Armenian Genocide (JCAG)

This is the right-wing counterpart of ASALA. Although smaller than ASALA, this group is capable of operations against Turkish interests around the world.

APPENDIX B

SOURCES OF INFORMATION

Special Reports and Publications

American Legion
Firing Line
P.O. Box 1055
Indianapolis, IN 46206

Anti-Defamation League of B'nai B'rith
823 United Nations Plaza
New York, NY 10017

Bureau of Public Affairs
U.S. Department of State
Washington, D.C. 20520

Corporate Consultants
P.O. Box 1134
Lenoir City, TN 37771

Criminal Justice Information Service
Box 6000
Rockville, MD 20850

Defense Technical Information Center
Cameron Station
Alexandria, VA 22314

National Institutes of Justice
Box 6000
Rockville, MD 20850

National Technical Information Center
5285 Port Royal Road
Springfield, VA 22161

Rand Corporation
P.O. Box 2138
Santa Monica, CA 90406-2138

Risks International
P.O. Box 115
Alexandria, VA 22313

Superintendent of Documents
U.S. Government Printing Office
Washington, D.C. 20402

T.V.I. Journal
P.O. Box 1055
Beverly Hills, CA 90213

U.S. Army Field Circular 100-37
For more information contact:
U.S. Army Terrorism Counteraction Office
Fort Leavenworth, KS 66027

Associations

American Society for Industrial Security
1655 North Fort Myer Drive
Arlington, VA 22209

Association of Former Intelligence Officers
6723 Whittier Avenue
Suite 303A
McLean, VA 22101

International Association of Bomb
   Technicians and Investigators
P.O. Box 6609
Colorado Springs, CO 80934

International Association of Chiefs of
   Police
P.O. Box 6010
Thirteen Firstfield Road
Gaithersburg, MD 20878

Tactical Response Association
P.O. Box 8413
Prairie Village, KS 66208

APPENDIX C

INSTALLATION VULNERABILITY-DETERMINING SYSTEM

The purpose of the Installation Vulnerability-Determining System (IVDS) is to provide a comparative measuring device to assess the vulnerability at a military installation. It was originally developed during the 1970s for the U.S. Army and has been modified here for more general use. For our purpose, any facility (for example, a manufacturing plant, an airport, an office building) can be considered an "installation." This version of the IVDS has been modified from the format included in TC 19-16, *Countering Terrorism on U.S. Army Installations.*

No factor should be a determinant in itself. The relationship between factors and their relevance to your specific situation must also be considered. The system uses a scale of 0 to 100 points. The higher your score, the higher your vulnerability.

As you use this system, avoid developing a "points mentality." Many facilities with a low point value are still primary targets for terrorists, whereas some facilities with a high point value may actually be low-priority targets. Remember to consider the results of the IVDS with respect to the results of your threat analysis. The threat analysis describes the immediate threat to your assets. The IVDS can be used to assess your vulnerability to that threat. The two assessments should be used together.

Each category has a paragraph on threat considerations. This may, in fact, be the most important part of the IVDS. This paragraph should be used to provide the team using the instrument with a thorough understanding of why and how the score is determined for each category. Typically, the IVDS would be completed by a small group of knowledgeable individuals and the results then presented to the threat management committee.

INSTALLATION CHARACTERISTICS AND SENSITIVITY (18 POINTS)

___ Very important persons (1 point per U.S. dignitary or star, 3 points per foreign dignitary) (6 points maximum)

___ Mission sensitivity (6 points maximum)

Nuclear, chemical, law enforcement facility (6 points)
Research and development facility (5 points)
International corporation or activity (4 points)
Domestic corporation or activity (2 points)

___ Current threat analysis conducted by law enforcement, military, or security professionals (available, 0 points; unavailable, 3 points)

___ Open access to facility (2 points), limited access (1 point), totally controlled access (0 points)

___ Symbolic value (shrine, museum, et cetera) (1 point)

COMMENT: All facilities should be capable of establishing and maintaining barrier integrity, especially in emergency situations.

THREAT CONSIDERATIONS:

_____

_____

_____

_____

_____

_____

_____

_____

_____

_____

_____

_____

_____

_____

_____

_____

STATUS OF TRAINING (12 POINTS)

___ No operational emergency operations center (EOC) and no counter-terrorism trained tactical team available (12 points)

___ Operational EOC, but no counterterrorism tactical team available (9 points)

___ Operational EOC, tactical team available but they do not have appropriate counterterrorism equipment or training (6 points)

___ Operational EOC, tactical team trained and equipped for counterterrorism operations (3 points)

___ Operational EOC, tactical team trained and equipped for counterterrorism operations and the system is tested at least every six months (0 points)

COMMENTS: Consideration must be given to establishing, equipping, maintaining, and testing of the EOC. The tactical team may be available from local law enforcement, security, or military assets.

THREAT CONSIDERATIONS:

_____

_____

_____

_____

_____

_____

_____

_____

_____

_____

_____

_____

_____

_____

_____

_____

_____

_____

AVAILABLE COMMUNICATIONS (10 POINTS)

__ Communications with lower elements only (4 points)

__ Communications with lower and lateral elements (3 points)

__ Communications with high, lower, and lateral units (0 points)

Land-Line Communications

__ Nondedicated (4 points)

__ Dedicated point-to-point (2 points)

__ Secure dedicated (0 points)

Radio

__ Nondedicated (2 points)

__ Dedicated (1 point)

__ Secure dedicated (0 points)

COMMENTS: Consideration should be given to security of lines of communication and the communications terminals at this facility. Secure radio communications are an important consideration for law enforcement, security, and military assets.

THREAT CONSIDERATIONS:

_____
_____
_____
_____
_____
_____
_____
_____
_____
_____
_____
_____
_____
_____
_____

AVAILABILITY OF LAW ENFORCEMENT RESOURCES (8 POINTS)

	RESPONSE TIME			
	1 hr	2 hr	3 hr	3 + hr
Trained, federal and local	1	2	3	4
Trained federal	2	3	4	5
Trained local	3	4	5	6
Nontrained local	4	5	6	7
Unavailable	8	8	8	8

COMMENTS: Consideration should be given to the determination of which law enforcement agencies are available, their resources, training status, and response time. Note that the term "federal" refers to U.S. and host country agencies.

THREAT CONSIDERATIONS:

_____

_____

_____

_____

_____

_____

_____

_____

_____

_____

_____

_____

_____

_____

_____

_____

_____

_____

_____

TIME AND DISTANCE FROM OTHER FACILITIES OR INSTALLATIONS ABLE TO LEND ASSISTANCE (7 POINTS)

TIME (hr)	DISTANCE (miles)			
	0–29	30–59	60–90	90+
$1\frac{1}{2}$	0	1	2	3
2	1	2	3	4
$2\frac{1}{2}$	2	3	4	5
3	3	4	5	6
3+	4	5	6	7

COMMENTS: Coordination should be made with the closest facility capable of providing assistance.

THREAT CONSIDERATIONS:

TIME AND DISTANCE FROM URBAN AREAS
(8 POINTS)

TIME (hr)	DISTANCE (miles)			
	0–59	60–89	90–120	120+
1	8	7	6	5
2	7	6	5	4
3	6	5	4	3
4	5	4	3	2
4+	4	3	2	1

COMMENTS: For purposes of this matrix, an urban area has a population in excess of 100,000 people. Because of their size, and the opportunity for the terrorists to blend into the population, urban areas offer the terrorist a safe haven conducive to conducting operations.

THREAT CONSIDERATIONS:

_____
_____
_____
_____
_____
_____
_____
_____
_____
_____
_____
_____
_____
_____
_____
_____
_____
_____
_____
_____

GEOGRAPHIC REGION (8 POINTS)

__ West Coast/Florida/outside the continental U.S. (8 points)
__ Eastern U.S. (6 points)
__ Southwest (4 points)
__ South, Northwest, Central, Northeast, and Mid-Atlantic (2 points)

COMMENTS: Points are awarded based on historical data gathered on terrorist activity by geographic region. This classification scheme must be modified according to the recent activities in your area.

THREAT CONSIDERATIONS:

_____
_____
_____
_____
_____
_____
_____
_____
_____
_____
_____
_____
_____
_____
_____
_____
_____
_____
_____
_____
_____
_____
_____
_____
_____

POPULATION DENSITY OF THE FACILITY OR INSTALLATION (8 POINTS)

POPULATION	AREA (square miles)		
	10–100	101–200	200+
50–500	3	2	1
500–2,500	6	5	4
2,500–5,000	8	7	6
5,000+	8	8	8

CONSIDERATIONS: For a facility located in an office complex, industrial park, et cetera, consider the population density for the entire immediate area.

THREAT CONSIDERATIONS:

_____

_____

_____

_____

_____

_____

_____

_____

_____

_____

_____

_____

_____

_____

_____

_____

_____

_____

_____

_____

_____

_____

PROXIMITY TO FOREIGN BORDERS (8 POINTS)

Mexican Border
__ 0–100 miles (8 points)
__ 101–500 miles (6 points)
__ More than 500 miles (2 points)

Canadian Border
__ 0–100 miles (6 points)
__ 101–500 miles (4 points)
__ More than 500 miles (2 points)

COMMENTS: If you are located outside of the U.S., assess the maximum point value.

THREAT CONSIDERATIONS:

_____
_____
_____
_____
_____
_____
_____
_____
_____
_____
_____
_____
_____
_____
_____
_____
_____
_____
_____
_____
_____
_____
_____

ACCESS TO THE FACILITY (8 POINTS)

Roads
__ Freeways or interstate highways (3 points)
__ Improved roads (2 points)
__ Secondary roads (1 point)

Airfields
__ Usable by high-performance (jet) aircraft (3 points)
__ Usable by low-performance (prop) aircraft (2 points)
__ Usable by small fixed-wing/rotary-wing aircraft (1 point)

Waterways
__ Navigable (2 points)
__ Nonnavigable (1 point)
__ None (0 points)

COMMENTS: Consideration should be given to these three methods of entering or exiting the facility both from the terrorists' point of view and from that of a law enforcement agency rendering assistance.

THREAT CONSIDERATIONS:

_____

_____

_____

_____

_____

_____

_____

_____

_____

_____

_____

_____

_____

_____

_____

TERRAIN (5 POINTS)

__ Built-up areas (5 points)
__ Mountainous, forested, or areas conducive to concealment (4 points)
__ Open areas (2 points)

COMMENTS: Terrain should be analyzed in conjunction with a review of facility sensitivity, adequacy of barrier fencing, and route of access and egress.

THREAT CONSIDERATIONS:

_____
_____
_____
_____
_____
_____
_____
_____
_____
_____
_____
_____
_____
_____

Total points for all 11 categories and compare your facility's total to the scale below. This will give you an idea of your overall vulnerability.

POINT TOTAL

0–10	Very low
11–30	Low
31–60	Medium
61–80	High
81–100	Very high

APPENDIX D

UNIT VULNERABILITY ASSESSMENT

The Unit Vulnerability Assessment Instrument (UVA) has been adapted from U.S. Army FC 100-37 and modified for general use. A unit is any special small group of people; the instrument is used to assess the vulnerability of this group when they are traveling to a designated area. The UVA is especially valuable if the group is traveling to a low-intensity conflict area.

The purpose of the UVA is to provide the person in charge of the unit with a tool to estimate the vulnerability of the group to a terrorist attack during deployment. The assessment must be continually updated while the unit is traveling and while it is located at its destination. The point value assessed by the instrument provides a subjective judgment of the degree of vulnerability, and these results should be considered along with the threat assessment and other available information.

For a deployment the assessment is divided into three parts:

- General Assessment
- Regional Assessment
- Specific Location Assessment

1. GENERAL ASSESSMENT
   A. Unit mission sensitivity
      ___ National security mission, highly publicized (6 points)
      ___ Sensitive mission, limited to medium publicity (3–5 points)
      ___ Covert or unpublicized mission (2 points)

B. VIPs
   — One point for each CEO or star (6 points maximum)
   — Diplomats or politicians (3 points)
C. Current threat analysis by intelligence agency or U.S. Department of State
   — Available (0 points)
   — Unavailable (3 points)
D. World attitude toward mission
   — General agreement (0 points)
   — General disagreement (3 points)
   — Add 1 point for stated disagreement by each of the following:
   Soviet Union
   Cuba
   North Korea
   Iran
   Libya
   Syria (6 points maximum)
E. Status of unit training
   — No terrorism security plan, no terrorism counteraction trained personnel (6 points)
   — Comprehensive security plans, terrorism counteraction trained personnel and teams (0 points)
F. Unity of security effort
   — Single unit or group with terrorism counteraction plan and organization (0 points)
   — Multiple groups or units. No coordinate plan (3 points)

2. REGIONAL ASSESSMENT
   A. Area of deployment
      — Europe, Middle East, Central/South America, Philippines (6 points)
      — Caribbean (4 points)
      — Other locations outside of continental United States (3 points)
   B. Country team guidance
      — Good intelligence, security advice or assistance, no conflicting mission (0 points)
      — No intelligence or security advice, conflicting mission (3 points)

C. Coordinated assistance from law enforcement or military agency
  __ Assistance immediately available (0 points)
  __ Assistance available within one hour (2 points)
  __ Assistance not available (3 points)

3. SPECIFIC LOCATION ASSESSMENT
  A. Availability of military, security, or law enforcement assistance
    __ On site (1 point)
    __ Thirty minutes reaction time (2 points)
    __ One hour reaction time (3 points)
  B. Location (separate assessment for each subunit separately located)
    __ Urban undefended (8 points)
    __ Urban semidefended (law enforcement or military) (4 points)
    __ Urban defended (perimeter fence, et cetera) (2 points)
    __ Rural undefended, close country (6 points)
    __ Rural undefended, open country (4 points)
    __ Rural defended (perimeter fence, et cetera) (2 points)
  C. Access to location
    __ Roads (3 points for freeways to 1 point for secondary roads) (3 points maximum)
    __ Airfields (3 points for high-performance aircraft to 1 point for small aircraft) (3 points maximum)
    __ Waterways (2 points for navigable to 1 point for nonnavigable) (2 points maximum)
  D. Personnel/vehicle access
    __ Free access to area (6 points)
    __ Access controlled by host nation (4 points)
    __ Access controlled by your organization (2 points)
    __ No unauthorized access allowed (0 points)
  E. Communications
    __ No outside communications (4 points)
    __ Communications with higher, lateral, and lower elements (0 points)
    __ Landline: 2 points for nondedicated, 0 points for secure dedicated (2 points maximum)
    __ Radio: 2 points for nondedicated, 0 points for semidedicated (2 points maximum)

F. Tactical limitations of law enforcement, military, or security personnel (rules of engagement)
   __ No live ammunition (6 points)
   __ No magazines in weapons (2 points)
   __ No outside patrols/operations/intelligence gatherings (4 points)
   __ No barricades or other methods of building hardening (6 points)
   __ Enforced stereotyped patterns of life (4 points)

APPENDIX E

CRISIS MANAGEMENT FILES

A separate crisis management file should be maintained on each person who is listed on your A list of potential personnel security risks. Files must be updated annually. The file should include photographs and/or videotapes of each person's residence, vacation house, and office area.

Date: _____

Employer: _____

Employee's Position: _____

	Name	Profile	Photo	Finger-prints	Writing Samples	Voice Tapes
Employee:	_____	____	____	_____	_____	____
Spouse:	_____	____	____	_____	_____	____
Children:	_____	____	____	_____	_____	____

Other family members living with employee:
Relationship

_____	_____	____	____	_____	_____	____
_____	_____	____	____	_____	_____	____
_____	_____	____	____	_____	_____	____
_____	_____	____	____	_____	_____	____
_____	_____	____	____	_____	_____	____

Other Information:

	Sketches	Photographs
Residence	____	_____
Second Residence	____	_____
Vehicle #1	____	_____
#2	____	_____

207

INDIVIDUAL PROFILE

Today's Date: _____

Name: _____

              Last   First   Middle

Nickname(s): _____

Social Security Number: _____

Driver's License: State _____ Number _____

Birth: Place _____ Date _____

Address: #1 _____

_____

_____

_____

_____

        #2 _____

_____

_____

_____

_____

Physical Description:

        Height _____Weight _____

        Hair _____ Eyes _____

        Eyeglasses _____ Hearing aid _____ Other _____

        Scars or Identifying Marks:

_____

_____

_____

_____

Special Medication Requirements: _____

_____

_____

_____

_____

_____

	Name	*Address*	*Telephone*
Physician:	_____	_____	_____
Dentist:	_____	_____	_____
Pharmacist:	_____	_____	_____

Name: _____

Profile of:

    Clubs or Organizations: _____

    _____

    _____

    _____

    Hobbies: _____

    _____

    _____

    Other Activities: _____

    _____

    _____

Routine Events:

    Sunday: _____

    Monday: _____

    Tuesday: _____

    Wednesday: _____

    Thursday: _____

    Friday: _____

    Saturday: _____

Bank(s): _____

    _____

    _____

Savings & Loan Association(s): _____

    _____

    _____

Credit Cards:

	Company	*Number*
1.	_____	_____
2.	_____	_____
3.	_____	_____
4.	_____	_____
5.	_____	_____
6.	_____	_____
7.	_____	_____

Name: _____
Vehicles: Include boats, campers, recreational vehicles

Make/Model	Year	Color	License	Vehicle ID

Other Relatives (not living with employee)

Relationship	Name	Address	Telephone
Father:			
Mother:			
Other:			

Children:
  Grade: _____
  School: _____
  Teachers: _____
Closest Friends:

Name	Address	Telephone

Comments:

Fingerprints

_____   _____
Thumb   Index
          Right Hand

                                        Staple
                                        Photograph
                                        Here

_____   _____
Thumb   Index
          Left Hand

Writing Sample: Please write the following sentence and sign using your
            regular signature.

"I feel good and am looking forward to tomorrow."

Sequence on Voice Tape: Number _____

APPENDIX F

PERSONAL, RESIDENTIAL, AND OFFICE AREA PROTECTION

This appendix has been adapted from publications available from the U.S. Government Accounting Office (GAO). Although the information was developed specifically for government employees, it is applicable to all personnel.

PERSONAL PROTECTION FOR THE EXECUTIVE

1. *Low profile.*
   Publicity should be kept to a minimum, and photographs of key personnel should not be easily obtainable. Other data that should be safeguarded includes information on family members, club or social memberships, residence locations, and travel plans.
2. *Routine.*
   Avoid patterns that are easily identified, including travel routes and arrival and departure times to and from work. Travel on well-populated and lighted public roadways.
3. *Recognition of surveillance.*
   If you think you are under surveillance, tell someone!
4. *Travel arrangements.*
   Advise family members or coworkers of your destinations and expected times of arrival. In a high-risk situation arrange for daily check ins.
5. *Code systems.*
   Have simple codes to alert family members or coworkers that something is wrong. You need different codes for each executive or traveler.

RESIDENTIAL AND FAMILY PROTECTION

1. *Family awareness.*
   All household members must develop a security awareness attitude. This does not mean that children and spouses should be made paranoid, but they must be aware of suspicious activities or occurrences.
2. *Pretexts or ruses.*
   All family members must adopt a questioning attitude toward persons seeking information or entry into a residence. This includes "distressed motorists" who may actually be criminals. Check identification and story before opening the door.
3. *Physical protective measures.*
   a. Door viewing. All exterior doors should be provided with a means of observing the caller from within.
   b. Door locks. Use chain-bolt locks where possible to allow door to be opened slightly while it is still secure. Consider double dead-bolt locks that require positive keying on both sides for all exterior doors.
   c. Windows. In high-risk situations, shutters or shatter-resistant materials should be used to increase window protection.
   d. Lighting. Outside lighting should illuminate the driveway and the area immediately around the residence. Electronic timers are used to insure that lights are turned on and off inside the house even if no one is home.
   e. Alarms. Alarm systems can provide a warning against attempted intrusions. However, remember that they are not a total defense and must be used in conjunction with locks, lighting, et cetera.
   f. Safe room. In high-risk situations a safe room may be justified. This is an internal room with a sturdy, solid door, heavy lock and hinges, and, if possible, a telephone or other outside communications capability.
4. *Unlisted telephone numbers.*
   Unlisted telephone numbers for residences are desirable. If this is not possible, list only the telephone number, not the address, in the telephone book.
5. *Emergency plans.*
   All family members should be aware of emergency telephone numbers. Distress codes and evacuation plans should also be prepared and rehearsed.

OFFICE AREA PROTECTION

1. *Office accessibility.*
   Offices of executives and others who may be at risk should be inaccessible to the general public. They should not be on the ground floor, and all windows facing public areas should be reinforced with bullet-resistant materials. All access to these areas should be monitored by a secretary or guard who screens *all* persons entering the area. All doors should lock from within and they should have panic bars and local annunciation.
2. *Alarm protection.*
   The point at which visitors enter the executive areas should be equipped with a hidden, unobtrusive means of activating an alarm. This alarm would notify individuals at the security office or guard center. The executive's desk should also be equipped with a hidden silent alarm.
3. *Visitor controls.*
   Controlled access and escorts for all visitors are essential elements in the security program. All unidentified visitors should be challenged. Visitors to the area should sign in and out, and identification should be required during the sign-in. Temporary badges should be issued to all visitors.
4. *After-hours access.*
   All personnel, including cleaning service people, should be cleared prior to entering these areas during nonworking hours. Guards should periodically inspect these areas during their after-hours tours. Inspections should be conducted on a random, unpredictable basis.
5. *Restrooms.*
   Executive restrooms and all other restrooms in the area should be locked at all times.
6. *Maintenance closets.*
   All maintenance closets and janitorial areas should be locked at all times. Keys should be issued only to authorized personnel.
7. *Telephone and electrical rooms.*
   Doors to telephone and electrical equipment rooms should be locked and keys issued only to authorized personnel.
8. *Executive office key controls.*
   Stringent lock and key control measures must be applied in the

executive office areas. This includes keys to all doors, desks, and filing cabinets.

9. *ID badges.*
The use of ID badges with a photograph of the individual and their signature is advised. Automated card readers and locks may also be employed to control access and record when access is obtained to restricted areas. All personnel should wear their badges while on the premises but remove them when they are off the premises.

10. *Fire protection.*
The facility should have a fire detection and suppression capability. Fire extinguishers should be readily available and checked periodically. Access to fire extinguishers by unauthorized personnel should be controlled.

11. *Safe room.*
An interior safe room for use by people who may be terrorist targets should be considered. It should be accessible from the outside, have a sturdy door and lock, and not be identifiable as a safe room. Emergency, first aid, and communications equipment should be kept there.

12. *Emergency supplies.*
Emergency supplies, including bomb blankets, should be stored at another location, in addition to those kept in the safe room.

13. *Publicity releases.*
All personal data on executives should be kept confidential, since this information may be used by terrorists to select victims.

14. *Incoming mail.*
Security awareness measures regarding incoming mail and packages is important. Identification checklists for possible letter and package bombs are included elsewhere in these materials. In high-threat situations the mail room should be equipped with special devices to inspect suspect items and a capability to isolate items that personnel suspect are explosives until explosive ordinance demolition (EOD) personnel arrive. Emergency telephone numbers to contact EOD teams should be posted in the mail room and at other strategic locations.

15. *Parking.*
Executive parking should not be conspicuously identified as such. Identify spaces with numbers or other codes (but no number one) rather than names.

16. *Travel plans.*

Information on travel itineraries and arrangements should not be publicized, but be restricted to as few people as possible. All written agendas and other correspondence regarding travel should be tightly controlled in the same manner as other sensitive company information.

APPENDIX G

SECURITY WHILE TRAVELING

This appendix is a checklist of actions you can take to reduce the probability of becoming a terrorist victim. The checklist was originally published by the International Association of Bomb Technicians and Investigators in cooperation with the Lockheed Missiles and Space Company, Inc. Copies of the pamphlet *Defusing the Threat* are available from the International Association of Bomb Technicians and Investigators, P.O. Box 6609, Colorado Springs, CO 80934.

General Travel Precautions

- Check with corporate security regarding potential problems in the countries you will visit.
- Restrict trip and itinerary information to close family and close business associates only.
- Use reliable hotels recommended by colleagues or the U.S. embassy or consulate.

Upon Arrival

- Maintain a low profile. Avoid any display of company affiliation when registering at the hotel.
- Ensure that locks on the hotel room doors are in working order.
- Do not leave identifying materials in the hotel room.
- Utilize the hotel vault or secure storage area for valuables.
- Avoid carrying large amounts of cash.
- Beware of friendly strangers.
- Avoid incidents such as civil unrest, demonstrations, crowds, fires, and accidents.

- Avoid actions identifying you as an American.
- Avoid establishing routine schedules.

Automobile Travel

- Keep vehicle in good working condition and know its capabilities. If possible, have a vehicle with an inside hood latch and locking gas cap.
- Keep gas tank at least half full at all times.
- Be sensitive to the possibility of surveillance.
- While driving, keep doors locked and windows open no more than two inches.
- Use well-traveled highways.
- Use the center lane on multilane highways to avoid being forced to the curb.
- Be alert to all signals, stop signs, and intersections.
- Be suspect of distress signals.
- Get around any suspicious roadblock by using the road shoulder or making a U-turn.
- Do not pick up strangers regardless of the circumstance.
- Use your rearview mirror frequently to check for following automobiles.
- Use the horn to attract help if you suspect you are being followed, and drive to a busy area of town where there is a local hospital, police, or fire station.
- Lock car when it is unattended.
- Separate the ignition key from other keys if you are leaving keys with a doorman or parking attendant.
- Park the car off the street at night.
- Report immediately any suspicious wires or packages.
- Avoid routines. Vary times and routes as well as your method of travel.
- Maintain a low profile with cabdrivers.
- Avoid using cabs for sight-seeing. Take bus tours instead.

Aircraft Travel

- Fly U.S. carriers whenever possible.
- When overseas, do not make reservations by telephone. Instead, go to the airport or a local office of the airline to purchase tickets.

- Leave early for the airport to minimize your exposure standing in long lines.
- Once in the terminal, move as quickly as possible to a secured area.

Hostage Survival Information

- Obey terrorist orders.
- Be courteous and polite to terrorists and other hostages.
- Do not debate, argue, or discuss political issues with terrorists or other hostages.
- Talk in a normal voice.
- Avoid abrupt movements.
- Locate yourself away from windows and doors if possible.
- Do not hesitate to answer questions unless your position or purpose of travel may pose a threat to the terrorists or their ideologies.
- Inform your captors if you have any special medical conditions or disabilities.
- Do not discuss possible retaliatory actions that may be taken by your family, friends, or company.
- Keep calm.

APPENDIX H

SAMPLE PHYSICAL SECURITY PLAN

This sample physical security plan has been extracted from FC 100-37-1/-OH 7-14.1, a U.S. Army publication. It can be adapted easily for use by a private organization or municipal government.

1. PURPOSE

   State purpose of the plan.

2. AREA SECURITY

   Define the areas, buildings, and other structures considered critical, and establish priorities for their protection.

3. CONTROL MEASURES

   Define and establish restrictions on access to and movement into critical areas. These restrictions can be categorized as personnel, materials, and vehicles.

   a. *Personnel Access.* Establish control pertinent to each area or structure.

      (1) Authority for access.

      (2) Access criteria for unit personnel, visitors, maintenance or support personnel, contractor personnel, and local police/armed forces.

      (3) Identification and control.

         (a) Description of the system to be used in each area. With a badge system, a complete description should be used to disseminate requirements for identification and control of personnel who conduct business on the installation.

         (b) Application of the system for unit personnel, visitors to

restricted or administrative areas, vendors, tradesmen, contractor personnel, and maintenance or support personnel.
b. *Material Control.*
  (1) Incoming.
    (a) Requirements for admission of material and supplies.
    (b) Inspection of material for possible sabotage hazards.
    (c) Special controls on delivery of supplies and/or personnel shipments in restricted areas.
  (2) Outgoing.
    (a) Documentation required.
    (b) Controls, as outlined above for incoming material control.
    (c) Classified shipments.
c. *Vehicle Control.*
  (1) Policy on registration of vehicles.
  (2) Policy on search of military and privately owned vehicles.
  (3) Parking regulations.
  (4) Controls for entering restricted and administrative areas.
    (a) Privately owned vehicles.
    (b) Military vehicles.
    (c) Emergency vehicles.
4. AIDS TO SECURITY
Indicate the manner in which the following aids to security will be implemented on the installation:
a. *Protective Barriers.*
  (1) Definition.
  (2) Clear zones.
    (a) Criteria.
    (b) Maintenance.
  (3) Signs.
    (a) Types.
    (b) Posting.
  (4) Gates.
    (a) Hours of operation.
    (b) Security requirements.
    (c) Lock security.
b. *Protective Lighting System.*
  (1) Use and control.
  (2) Inspection.

(3) Pointing inward or outward.
(4) Action to be taken during a commercial power failure.
(5) Action to be taken during an alternate source of power failure.
(6) Emergency lighting systems.
    (a) Stationary.
    (b) Portable.
c. *Intrusion-Detection Systems.*
(1) Security classification.
(2) Inspection.
(3) Use and monitoring.
(4) Action to be taken in event of alarm conditions.
(5) Maintenance.
(6) Alarm logs or registers.
(7) Sensitivity settings.
(8) Fail-safe and tamperproof provisions.
(9) Monitor panel location.
d. *Communications.*
(1) Locations.
(2) Use.
(3) Tests.
(4) Authentication.

5. INTERIOR GUARD PROCEDURES
Include general instructions that apply to all interior guard personnel (fixed and mobile). Detailed instructions such as special orders and SOP's should be attached as annexes. Ensure that randomness is incorporated in guard procedures.
a. *Composition and Organization.*
b. *Tour of Duty.*
c. *Essential Posts and Routes.*
d. *Weapons and Equipment.* Live ammunition? Magazines on weapons? Round in the chamber?
e. *Training.*
f. *Use of Sentry/Patrol Dogs.*
g. *Method of Challenging with Sign and Countersign.*
h. *Rules of Engagement.*
i. *Alert Force.*
(1) Composition.
(2) Mission.
(3) Weapons and equipment.

(4) Location.

(5) Deployment concept.

6. CONTINGENCY PLANS

Indicate required actions in response to various emergency situations. Detailed plans such as counterterrorism, bomb threats, hostage negotiation, disaster, and fire should be attached as annexes.

a. *Individual Actions.*

b. *Alert Force Actions.*

c. *Security Alert Status.*

7. SECURITY ALERT STATUS

8. USE OF AIR SURVEILLANCE

9. COORDINATING INSTRUCTIONS

a. *Integration with Plans of Host or Nearby Military Installations.*

b. *Liaison and Coordination.*

(1) Local civil authorities.

(2) Federal agencies.

(3) Military organizations.

APPENDIX I

BOMB THREAT FORMS

These forms are from *Bomb Threats and Search Techniques,* a pamphlet published by the Department of the Treasury, Bureau of Alcohol, Tobacco, and Firearms (BATF). For copies of the complete pamphlet, contact your nearest BATF office or the U.S. Government Printing Office, Washington, D.C.

Suggested form to be completed by investigators following
BOMB THREAT CALLS
Type of Complainant:
☐ School   ☐ Hospital   ☐ Industrial manufacturing company
☐ Business   ☐ Other
Business name of complainant _____
Business address _____
Business telephone _____
Name of person reporting complaint _____
Telephone number that call was received on _____
Date and time of call _____
Name of person who talked to the caller _____
Exact words said by caller _____
Background noises (street sounds, baby crying, et cetera) _____
Information about caller: Age ___ Sex ___ Race ___ Accent ____ Educational level _____
Speech impediments (drunk, lisp, et cetera) _____
Attitude (calm, excited, et cetera) _____
Any suspects? ☐ Yes   ☐ No _____

Have previous calls been received?   If yes, approximately how many?
☐ Yes   ☐ No _____
Has the telephone company security department been notified?
☐ Yes   ☐ No
Was any incendiary or explosive device found?
☐ Yes   ☐ No
Number of threats received thus far during calendar year _____

CHECKLIST WHEN YOU RECEIVE A BOMB THREAT
Time and date reported: _____
How reported: _____
Exact words of caller: _____
_____
_____
_____

Questions to ask: _____
1. When is bomb going to explode? _____
2. Where is bomb right now? _____
3. What kind of bomb is it? _____
4. What does it look like? _____
5. Why did you place the bomb? _____
6. Where are you calling from? _____
Description of caller's voice: _____
Male ___ Female ___ Young ___ Middle-aged ___ Old ___ Accent ___
Tone of voice _____ Background noise _____ Is voice familiar? _____
If so, who did it sound like? _____
_____
Other voice characteristics: _____
Time caller hung up: _____ Remarks: _____
_____
_____
_____
_____
Name, address, telephone number of recipient: _____
_____
_____
_____

RECORD:

1. Date _____ and time _____ of call.
2. Exact words spoken: _____
_____
_____
_____
_____
_____

3. ☐ Male   ☐ Female
   ☐ Adult   ☐ Child
   Estimated age: _____ Race: _____

4. Speech (check applicable boxes)
   ☐ Slow   ☐ Excited   ☐ Disguised
   ☐ Rapid   ☐ Loud   ☐ Broken
   ☐ Normal   ☐ Normal   ☐ Sincere
   Accent: _____

5. Background noises: _____
_____
_____
_____
_____
_____

6. Name of person receiving the call: _____

NOTES

CHAPTER ONE

1. FC 100-37 *Terrorism Counteraction,* U.S. Army Combined Arms Center, Fort Leavenworth, KS, July 1987.
2. For more information, request a copy of *Patterns of Global Terrorism: 1987* from the U.S. Department of State or the U.S. Government Printing Office.
3. From a captured Iranian document.
4. TC 19-16 *Countering Terrorism on U.S. Army Installations,* Headquarters TRADOC, Fort Monroe, VA, April 1983.
5. Ibid.
6. Ibid.
7. For more information, see Brian M. Jenkins (Ed.), *Terrorism and Personal Protection.* Stoneham, MA: Butterworth Publishers, 1985.
8. James Adams, *The Financing of Terror.* New York: Simon and Schuster, 1986.
9. For more information on the chemical-biological terrorist threat, see Richard C. Clark, *Technological Terrorism.* Old Greenwich, CT: The Devin-Adair Company, 1980, and J. D. Douglas and N. C. Livingston, *America the Vulnerable.* New York: Lexington Books, 1987.
10. *The Terror Trade: Buying the Bomb.* Videotape available from the Better World Society, Inc., 1988.

CHAPTER TWO

1. *Public Report of the Vice President's Task Force on Combatting Terrorism* (VP Task Force Report). Washington, DC: U.S. Government Printing Office, 1986.
2. Definition according to U.S. State Department terrorism report in 1983. The agency has since modified its definition.
3. Current definitions used by the Department of Defense and other U.S. government agencies.
4. VP Task Force Report.

CHAPTER THREE

1. William Powell, *The Anarchist Cookbook.* Secaucus, NJ: Lyle Stuart, Inc., 1971.

2. Newspaper interview with General Kelly, former commandant of the U.S. Marine Corps.

3. Unpublished report on airline hijackings.

4. Ibid.

5. For information and other examples, see Brian M. Jenkins (Ed.), *Terrorism and Personal Protection*. Stoneham, MA: Butterworth Publishers, 1985.

6. J. D. Douglas and N. C. Livingston, *America the Vulnerable*. New York: Lexington Books, 1987.

7. Selection criteria are derived from several different sources and are based on interviews with terrorist leaders.

CHAPTER FOUR

1. For additional information, see U.S. Army FM 19-30 *Physical Security* or TC 19-16 *Countering Terrorism on U.S. Army Installations*. Crime prevention checklists are also available from most major law enforcement agencies.

2. Brian M. Jenkins (Ed.), *Terrorism and Personal Protection*. Stoneham, MA: Butterworth Publishers, 1985.

3. Information is available in the *Anarchist Handbook* and is also found in several publications written by Scott French and others that are available through mail order book publishers.

4. Steven Fink, *Crisis Management*. New York: AMACOM, 1986.

5. *The Urban Guerrilla* is a publication that was available during the 1970s from the active support structure of the New World Liberation Front.

CHAPTER FIVE

1. Sources include U.S. Army Regulation 525-13 *The Army Terrorism Counteraction Program*. Washington, DC: Headquarters Department of the Army, 1988, and Anthony J. Scotti, *Executive Safety & International Terrorism*. Englewood Cliffs, NJ: Prentice-Hall, Inc., 1986.

2. For additional information, see the criminal indictments for members of the Brotherhood of Silence, prepared by the U.S. Department of Justice.

3. From a special 1986 television production, CBS Reports, "Terrorism: War in the Shadows" with Walter Cronkite.

4. *FALN: Threat to America*. Alexandria, VA: Western Goals, 1981.

5. Adapted from a list prepared at the U.S. Army Military Intelligence School, Fort Huachuca, Arizona.

6. U.S. Army TC 19-16 *Countering Terrorism on U.S. Army Installations*.

7. U.S. Army FC 100-37 *Terrorism Counteraction*.

8. U.S. Army Regulation 525-13, *The Army Terrorism Counteraction Program.*

CHAPTER SIX

1. FM 34-60 *Counterintelligence.* Headquarters Department of the Army, August 1985.
2. U.S. Army Regulation AR 530-1 *Operations Security.* 15 October 1985.
3. TC 19-16 *Countering Terrorism on U.S. Army Installations.*

CHAPTER SEVEN

1. For more information, see Brian M. Jenkins (Ed.), *Terrorism and Personal Protection.* Stoneham, MA: Butterworth Publishers, 1985.
2. For more information, see Anthony J. Scotti, *Executive Safety & International Terrorism.* Englewood Cliffs, NJ: Prentice-Hall, 1986.
3. The account of Sir Geoffrey Jackson has been published in a number of books and articles.
4. FM 34-60 *Counterintelligence.* Headquarters Department of the Army, August 1985.
5. For more information, see TC 19-16 *Countering Terrorism on U.S. Army Installations.*
6. *Bomb Threat and Search Techniques,* Department of the Treasury, Bureau of Alcohol, Tobacco, and Firearms, 1988.

CHAPTER EIGHT

1. FM 19-30 *Physical Security.* Headquarters Department of the Army, 1979.
2. Ibid.
3. Ibid.

CHAPTER NINE

1. FM 100-37 *Terrorism Counteraction.* Headquarters Department of the Army, July 1987.

2. Unpublished report.

3. *Bomb Threat and Search Techniques*. Department of the Treasury, Bureau of Alcohol, Tobacco, and Firearms, 1988.

4. For more information, see Brian M. Jenkins (Ed.), *Terrorism and Personal Protection*. Stoneham, MA: Butterworth Publishers, 1985.